Advance Praise for
Suspended by No String

"Peter Himmelman's songs and music have been my source of inspiration in the past two decades. *Suspended by No String* now takes us to the magical world of poetry and, with merciless honesty, transforms, elevates, and cuts deeply into every mundane bastion of reality. Warmly recommended!"
— **Judea Pearl**, Turing Prize winner, author of *The Book of Why*, and Professor of Computer Science at UCLA

"A soulful, beautiful, melancholy, joyful and redemptive journey with a creative genius of the heart. This is a prayer book, a hymnal, a sacred text you will revisit again and again."
— **Steve Leder**, *New York Times* bestselling author of *The Beauty of What Remains* and *For You When I Am Gone*

"Peter Himmelman has been a lifelong inspiration to me. In *Suspended by No String*, he shows us how we can embrace the joyful, open-hearted curiosity that truly feeds the soul."
— **Peggy Orenstein**, *New York Times* bestselling author of *Boys & Sex, Girls & Sex*, and *Cinderella Ate My Daughter*

"Every time one picks up a book, we hope that it will change us in some way. Like a great song or painting, we hope that it will make us feel something intensely enough to make us see the world in a different way, and to carry ourselves through the world in a new way. As Kafka said, "a book should be an axe for the frozen sea within us." With his simple and thoughtful honesty, Peter accomplishes this kind of effect with this book. It sent me down roads that I hadn't walked down for years. It made me sad, regretful, thoughtful, and made me remember things from ~~my life that I had~~ tucked into the reliquary of lost memories we can ask for when we pick up a book. It does all of this without being effortful or forced. Read it and let yourself go to places that you haven't visited for years. It just might change you for a little while; an hour, a day, or even more."

— **Larry Klein**, multi-Grammy-winning producer, songwriter, and musician

"Peter Himmelman has a great gift for helping us open our minds, discover new ideas, and express ourselves."

— **Jonathan Eig**, Pulitzer Prize–winning author of *King*, *Ali*, *Capone*, and *Luckiest Man*

"A walking, living, breathing inspiration to many, Peter Himmelman embodies spirit, wit, song, and faith in a cool and seamless fashion. *Suspended by No String* captures this kaleidoscopic energy in so many diverse and delightful ways. It is guaranteed to uplift, galvanize, and propel the reader towards a no-strings-attached life, suspended by success."

— **Simon Jacobson**, *New York Times* bestselling author of *Toward a Meaningful Life*

"In a time of relentless information, it feels like we've lost the ability to appreciate the mystical. In *Suspended by No String*, Peter Himmelman shows us how to recapture the mystic in a tangible way. By putting hand to musical instrument, pen to paper, and thought to action, we can become a little bit holy. And in these times, as in every other time, a little bit of holy is beautifully mortal."

— **Sherman Alexie**, poet, bestselling author, winner of the PEN/Faulkner Award for Fiction

"The creative mind of Peter Himmelman is illuminated through the lens of his philosophical and existential reflections in this fascinating blend of memoir, personal journal, and self-help inquiry.

Our fascinating guide's 'notes to self' are an invitation to ask ourselves fundamental questions about life and death, the meaning of experience, and how to awaken our own minds to address these important foundations of our time, here in these material bodies, on this journey of life on Earth."

— **Daniel J. Siegel, MD**, *New York Times* bestselling author of *IntraConnected*, *Mind*, and *Aware*

"Peter Himmelman is one of the most talented, smartest, coolest cats I know (or 'Katz,' depending on where you grew up). The breadth of his knowledge, interests, and curiosity is a remarkable thing, and here he has tapped it all to concoct this delicious, fun-to-read, inspiring, spiritual soup. Grab a spoon and dive in. I promise you, only good will come from reading this."

— **Paul Reiser**, comedian, actor, and *New York Times* bestselling author

"Peter Himmelman's latest book, *Suspended by No String*, pushes us toward believing in the innate spiritual capacities we often lock away out of fear of falling short of our dreams."

— **Mike Sullivan**, retired US Army colonel

"In *Suspended by No String*, Peter Himmelman manages to synthesize his experiences as an extraordinary musician and songwriter, his faith, and some hard-earned life lessons into a stunningly simple yet profound collection, which will awaken anyone and everyone's innate spirituality."

— **Steve Berlin**, producer, saxophonist with Los Lobos

"Music is a form of prayer, a language that speaks of the heart's deepest desire, and Peter Himmelman is that rare *neshama* [soul] who can translate the ineffable into the practical."

— **Ben Sidran**, internationally acclaimed jazz musician and author

SUSPENDED BY NO STRING

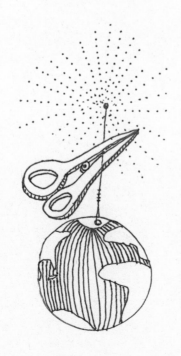

SUSPENDED BY NO STRING

A Songwriter's Reflections on
Faith, Aliveness, and Wonder

PETER HIMMELMAN

A REGALO PRESS BOOK
ISBN: 979-8-88845-483-1
ISBN (eBook): 979-8-88845-484-8

Cover Design by Jim Villaflores
Illustrations by Peter Himmelman

Publishing Team:
Founder and Publisher – Gretchen Young
Editorial Assistant – Caitlyn Limbaugh
Managing Editor – Madeline Sturgeon
Production Manager – Alana Mills
Production Editor – Rachel Hoge
Associate Production Manager – Kate Harris

This is a work of nonfiction. All people, locations, events, and situations are portrayed to the best of the author's memory.

As part of the mission of Regalo Press, a donation is being made to Magen David Adom, as chosen by the author.

Regalo Press
New York • Nashville
regalopress.com

Published in the United States of America
1 2 3 4 5 6 7 8 9 10

For Maria, with whom life has become
indescribably more beautiful

On the day I come to the edge of my language,
it won't be because there's nothing more to say.
It will be because there's too much to say.

A little light dispels much darkness.

—Schneur Zalman of Liadi

CONTENTS

Author's Note..1

Introduction 3

PART I: ASTONISHMENTS

Still on the Road 9

Becoming Sacred..10

No Small Beauty 16

Wailing Wall, Jerusalem, 1968.........................18

The Battle of the Two Souls..............................20

Last Thoughts 22

Starlings 24

People, Power, Prayer..26

We See the Bird...29

Everything 30

The Spaceship...33

How Much? 35

A Strongly Held Belief 37

Job Descriptions..38

Adjustments 40

99.9 to 0.1 42

The Big Canvas 45

The Least Among Us 47

Saga of the Miraculous Talking Bear....................48

Window Cleaner 59

Morning...61

Being Human...62

5 Percent Words 63

First Things First 65

Expansions 67

Difficulties 69

Siblings 71

Reminder 72

At the Moment of the Emergence of Stars...........73

PART II: SHADOWS

Susie..77

Mea Culpa 83

Beneath the Crust 85

Nothing to Say..87

Visiting 88

Compassion 89

Suspended by No String 90

Afternoon Prayer..94

Rational 95

Circles...96

A Strange Small Sense of Elation 98

Letter to an Unknown Address.......................... 100

Rows of Silence 102

Learning from Experience 103

Possible 104

The Howling of Coyotes.................................... 106

Tom Petty, 1983.. 109

Nighttime Prayer 111

Shovel 113

Brave Face 114

Logging the Distance 115

Down to the Bluffs... 117

Outsize Joy... 119

White Coats for the Pines 121

Heavy Leather Bag 123

How Lost Can One Man Be? 126

Untroubled Days... 127

At the Center of the World 129

Split Screen 131

Prayer for a Morning with Many Shadows 133

Sunset 135

PART III: TEACHERS

Woman with the Strength of Ten Thousand Men........... 139

Blues Singer.. 151

Effortlessly 156

Freedom in Restriction...................................... 159

What God Is Not.. 163

Rocks Don't Fly... 164

Knowing 165

The Man in the Dirty Shroud............................. 170

On the Other Side 172

The Delicate Indestructibility of Love 173

Wishing You Were Someplace Else 175

Seven Qualities Found Only in God 177

Amen 178

Earring, 1976 180

Murder on the Second Road 181

Winged Words 183

Stuff We "Know" 185

What in the World Is Certain About the World? 188

Spaces in a Fast of Words 191

On a Bus Ride to Denver 193

Pressure Washer 197

Cracks 199

A Turning Point 200

The Insufficiency of Words 205

Watching My Brother Fly 207

Homecoming 210

Canoe, 1972 213

Called to Attention 215

Choices 218

The Best Kind of School by Far 221

A for Awake 223

Drive-In Movie 230

Acknowledgments 233

About the Author 235

AUTHOR'S NOTE

It may seem strange that in a book about faith, I deliberated over whether to use the word "God." But for many people, including a few of my friends and family members, "God" is a loaded term. For some of them, it's also a politicized term, even a dangerous one. Through their negative experiences with "organized" religion, they have reasonably concluded that belief in God is little more than a crutch or a childish fantasy.

I discussed my decision to use the word with several such individuals. The comments I got were mostly along these lines: "Peter, you're going to alienate a lot of potential readers, particularly those with a high level of education and sophistication." I've also heard this: "People don't want to hear about God; it's too religious. Can't you talk about spirituality instead? Wouldn't that be less off-putting?"

I had a few comments of my own. For example: Why is spirituality, which is itself an irrational and decidedly mystical idea, any more acceptable to a so-called rational person than God? I've heard people beseeching the "universe" for help with business decisions, weight loss, and romantic relationships, as if the universe possesses a power that God lacks—as if praying to the universe is logical but praying to God is not.

There's an age-old Chassidic joke that addresses this well.

A rabbi is walking to synagogue to pray on Yom Kippur, the most important holiday in Judaism, a day on which the use of fire is prohibited. On his way he sees a congregant smoking a pipe. The rabbi asks, "Are you aware that smoking is prohibited today?" The congregant says, "Yes, I'm aware of the prohibition, but I don't believe in God." To which the rabbi calmly answers, "I understand completely. The same God you don't believe in I also don't believe in."

Of course, because both God and spirituality transcend the physical, neither can ever be proved or disproved. But there is one thing I *am* certain of: the preponderance of evidence that I've accumulated over my lifetime has convinced me that it is simply more plausible to conclude that God exists.

I'm looking out my window right now: the leaves of the maple trees are turning a dark crimson; the hawks are swooping down into the field to catch a fat rabbit or a squirrel; the clouds are gray and heavy in the stillness of a foreboding sky. I ask myself, *How could this possibly be happening through what Einstein called "a roll of the dice"?* Perhaps it's because I've been a creator for most of my life that I find it so difficult to perceive of a universe without God.

INTRODUCTION

Every songwriter needs three things: a pen to write with, an instrument to play on, and a pair of extra-sensitive antennae with which to home in on the joy, the anguish, and the mystery of being alive. I keep those things handy because I'm a songwriter by trade, one who has a uniquely devoted audience. That audience seems to appreciate the many songs of mine that ponder the bewildering miracle of humanity's dual earthbound and spiritual nature as well as the tension and apparent contradiction this implies.

Along with composing, performing, and recording songs, I've been teaching songwriting for more than three decades. I don't just teach the mechanics of songwriting—the construction of verses and choruses, when and how to apply harmonic shifts, and how to find creative freedom within the strict architecture of various musical structures—I also try to coax from my students the "why" of their songs. I'm interested to know what's at the heart of what aspiring writers want to say, not just in a commercial or utilitarian sense but also in a spiritual sense. To me, the best songs have always been part engineering and part benediction.

I'll often ask my students to describe how they might feel about their body of work if they had left this world and were able to look down at the effect their songs have had on listeners. I want to impress upon them that music can be a *sacred* thing—a thing set apart from all others—and that their songs, while still very much part of the physical world, are potential conduits to the unseen world of the spirit. In that same way, this collection of stories and reflections is a lot like the many records I've released over the course of thirty-five years.

I didn't write my songs to achieve any specific outcome, but as I look back at the bulk of them, it occurs to me that I might have unwittingly conjured them up as prayers—prayers of love, prayers of remembrance, prayers to ward off loneliness, prayers to awaken hope, and prayers to ease the pain of knowing that some answers will never be found. And just as my songs vary in tempo, tone, and length, so, too, do the narrative reflections I share with you in the following pages. Like most things in my life, my definition of faith is a work in progress, so it tends not to be overly rigid. And yet it remains a powerful, maybe the most powerful, factor in the way I move through the world.

◻ ◻ ◻

This book is structured in three parts: "Astonishments" contains recollections of my experiences, insights, and imaginings, which even in their apparent insignificance have moved me to such a degree that they have reframed my conception of the world. The part called "Shadows" examines the pain that hides in a sealed vault inside my storehouse of memories. I wouldn't wish this pain on anyone, and yet I wouldn't trade it for anything. In "Teachers," I ask: Who are my teachers? What do I owe them? What is the value of the gifts they've given, whether they know I've received them or not? It's impossible to say. I only know that if I had never encountered these people, I would be something far less than I've become. In each of the sections you'll also encounter "Notes to Self," which are some of the things I frequently have to remind myself of. They include my doubts, my small and very personal epiphanies, my joy over having rediscovered my faith—and my consternation when it occasionally goes missing.

Feel free to dip into *Suspended by No String* occasionally or read it in one shot. There's no plot, no through line, and no surprise ending, so don't be dismayed if you don't find one. What I do hope you'll find, whether you consider yourself a spiritual person, a religious person, or an avowed atheist, is a stronger connection to the part of you that is always curious, always hopeful, and always filled with music and light.

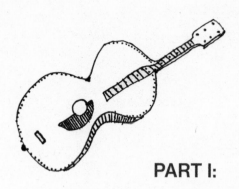

PART I:

ASTONISHMENTS

Chord suggestion: Cadd9

When you're writing a song, try to recall things that moved you to laughter or tears. It's best to keep your intellect out of the process. It will only impede your spirit from having its say.

STILL ON THE ROAD

Returning home any time soon is impossible.
We are spirits after all, sent down to inhabit delicate
bodies. Bodies that for all our efforts remain tethered
to a desire for the fleeting things.

One day, we think,
we will sate this unbearable hunger,
slake this unbearable thirst.

We are staggering angels, forever on a quest to unveil
the point of our sojourns.
The difficulty of our doing so lies in the fact that each
day we move through a place and time, which swears
that there never was a point
—and that there will never be one.

This notion is especially difficult for those of us, who
are still on the road, still dreaming up songs
to tell the world otherwise.

BECOMING SACRED

The saddest song I ever heard was the one I learned from my Grandma Rose. Never was there a Delta blues or an Irish lament more melancholy, more genuinely haunting than that Yiddish folk song. The song was composed, if that's even the right word, by a young mother, a neighbor of Grandma Rose, who for half a loaf of bread and a pear hired her to watch over her ailing child while she prepared the simple lentil stew that she would later sell in the marketplace of the small shtetl. The young mother's husband had died of tuberculosis only days before. And now the infant daughter lay in a small wooden cradle, the tiny girl herself just days or hours from death at the hand of the same sickness.

Grandma Rose was nine years old at the time, listening as the young mother sang the mournful tune. The song never had an actual title. We all just called it "Einschlafe, Mein Kindt," after its first words.

Einschlafe, mein kindt, deine eigilach un schluf... (Sleep, my child, close your eyes and sleep...).

That tragic relic of a long-forgotten Romanian shtetl was likely the first song I ever knew. It was what Grandma Rose would sing to me and my three siblings before bed, while bathing us, and in all manner of quiet moments.

Grandma Rose came to America on an aging merchant steamship at the age of twelve with her brother, my great-uncle Sol, who was ten. For those of us who soar across continents while watching first-run movies and sipping Chardonnay in the comfort and safety of a modern airliner, the enormity of that perilous trip is impossible to comprehend. Sailing alone for weeks on end surely left terrible scars on those two dirt-poor siblings from the western shores of the Black Sea.

Perhaps that's why Grandma Rose never ventured far from her extended family or from her small circle of Yiddish-speaking friends. And although she'd lived in America for more than seventy years and spoke English reasonably well, I never once heard her tell a story that didn't contain at least some Yiddish. The story I remember most vividly was the gruesome one—the one about the people who took ill and died aboard that steamship, a speck of steel and smoke traversing the Atlantic. The crew would wrap the newly dead in canvas—mostly old people who had succumbed to the rigors of the trip, but sometimes young children, too—then Grandma Rose would watch them lift the bodies off the deck and heave them over the side.

It's 1974. My jeans and ski jacket are bulging. I've just stolen six feet of plastic tubing and some Pyrex beakers from the eighth-grade chemistry lab, hoping to create the world's most elaborate hookah pipe. On my way downstairs to my bedroom, I pass Grandma Rose in the kitchen as she sits upright at the table chopping vegetables into tiny pieces—green and red peppers, eggplant, and Spanish onion. "Are you hungry, *mein tir'e kindt*? I'm making *potli'jel*," she calls out.

"No thanks, Grandma," I say. "I'm going downstairs for a while; I've got a lot of homework to do." Stopping to eat Romanian eggplant with my grandma is the last thing on my mind.

I place a copy of Neil Young's *After the Gold Rush* on the turntable and set to work on my monster pipe. After it meets my meager standard of excellence, I reach up into my closet, move some of the sweaters from the top shelf, and pop loose the ceiling tile that I use to conceal my ever-dwindling stash of Minnesota green. I open the window above my bed, fire up the hookah, and let the smoke drift out into the backyard. Twenty minutes of water-cooled splendor later, I get high—unusually high—and I drift back upstairs to find Grandma Rose still busy, chopping her vegetables and humming quietly to herself.

I wait in the kitchen, staring at her now, the sun streaming through the back door and casting light on her busy hands. I'm struck by how old she looks. I notice her hair first, whitish-gray and sparse, then the deep creases on her cheeks. I'm suddenly aware that someone I love very much will one day, and likely very soon, pass on to the world of spirits.

I stand back where she can't see me and watch as if seeing her for the first time. I feel something of the chain of generations working its way up from the shadowy reaches of my subconscious, a chain to which I belong and that stretches far into the past, even as far back as biblical times. Grandma

Rose is no longer the old woman who shows up at our home speaking words I don't understand and preparing foods I don't especially care for. She is the beautiful, lively daughter of the Romanian shtetl, the birthplace of my people. She is the beloved and tender child of a man and a woman I've never met, and they are in turn the children of people I've never met—and the chain goes back and back. I, too, am part of that chain. I feel that now.

Though I live in a place called Saint Louis Park, Minnesota, a place that never had a whisper of meaning to me beyond the fact that my friends live close by, all the things I've taken for granted until now have been abruptly transformed. The crab apple trees outside our window, just beyond where Grandma Rose is now, their branches heavy with tiny tart apples, reach upward and outward like men in prayer. The passenger jets that fly directly above our small house are no longer the product of science and engineering; they are soaring projections of the human imagination. Nothing about our kitchen is normal; nothing about my shoes or my clothing is normal; nothing about the Volkswagen parked in our driveway is normal. And at the table, Grandma Rose, who by her very presence has set this strange new reality ablaze, continues to chop her vegetables and hum to herself. Surely she must know all this. Surely she must have once had these same conflicting feelings—of being part of something and yet exquisitely lonely, of being at home and yet frighteningly lost. Grandma Rose, whom I'd never paid nearly enough attention, does indeed know these things.

When she asks, *"Peter, vilst du a bissel potli'jel mit coilige?"* (Peter, do you want a little eggplant on a piece of challah?) I experience an overwhelming sensation of compassion and sadness. "No, thanks," I say. And as easily as I take my next breath, I hear the Yiddish song coming from who knows where. I had neither heard it nor thought about it even once in many years. It's a fragment of a childhood dream, but distinct now, like a sense memory from the time when I first waded into the warm, still shallows of Lake Calhoun.

"Grandma," I ask, "can you…would you sing me that song again? The Yiddish one that you always used to sing?" Her face brightens. She puts down her paring knife and begins to sing the song several times over in her soft, wavering soprano. I grab a pen and paper to capture the moment with a transcription of the song's lyrics, hurrying to preserve this precious piece of my past.

When the singing ends, Grandma Rose looks pleased. She leaves the table and goes to the phone to call her brother Sol. The conversation is entirely in Yiddish, and yet somehow I'm able to understand each word. I take the paper with the words to the Yiddish song in both my hands. I hold it up to the beam of sunlight where Grandma Rose had just been sitting. It feels as if it were a page taken from the Torah itself. Sacred words, sacred past—sacred light.

□ □ □

Not long after that afternoon, Grandma Rose began to lapse into senility. My mother would often call on me to sing

"Einschlafe" to her, as if to pull her back from wherever it was that her ageless spirit was moving toward. Hearing me sing it made her sit up slightly, made her eyes seem less dim.

Sometimes, she even mouthed the words.

Einschlafe, mein kindt, deine eigilach un schluf... (Sleep, my child, close your eyes and sleep...).

NO SMALL BEAUTY
(NOTE TO SELF)

You sometimes feel as though you exist inside a snow globe. Life is happening to you, but at one remove. You are touching it, but through the walls of a glass bubble. Voices sound like static instead of meaningful communication. And the things you see, whether during your waking hours or in your dreams, have lost their definite outlines.

Exactly when this dullness of heart overtook you, you have no idea. Like many things, it happened without your noticing it and without your understanding it. Yet at some point, you began to accept it as a kind of cosmic test, a test of your will and your faith. You wisely filed that experience under "things I will never understand." And while that isn't the resolution you'd once wished for, it is surprisingly gratifying now.

Being able to relax your hold on the mountain of things you once found too burdensome to carry is an unexpected pleasure. In fact, it's become a thing of no small beauty. Instead of circumscribing your sense of the world, letting go of your need to know has broadened it. You have given yourself permission to fully accept that divine intelligence is not for you or any mortal to comprehend.

When you were a boy, your father explained to you that the people a painter creates with his brush have no more ability to comprehend the painter than you have to comprehend God. This, you think, makes sense in a way it never did when you were a child.

WAILING WALL,
JERUSALEM, 1968

I'm with my dad and my brother, Paul, at the Wailing Wall. It's weird to think that only a week ago I was at home watching reruns of *Gilligan's Island* and looking for my dad's Japanese *Playboy*s in the bottom drawer of his bedroom dresser during the commercials. Now I'm in Jerusalem, in the glaring sun beneath this gigantic wall of stone. When I'm sure no one's looking, I put both hands on the wall, then I touch my forehead to it. The stones are colder than you'd think they'd be in all this heat.

For reasons I don't understand, I start to cry. I'd be embarrassed if Paul or my dad saw me like this, so I pretend I'm praying. I wonder, though: *Am I just crying because people are supposed to cry here? If the rabbis at my Hebrew school had shown me pictures of some bridge in Saint Paul, would I have cried at that, too?*

Sometimes, I cry for God. I don't picture God as an old, bearded guy or anything like that. I just think of Him as...I don't know, maybe like a baby. A really powerful but helpless little baby who's always lonely because He's been left in charge of everything—every snowflake and every whale, every single drop of water in the ocean. Who's He got as a friend? He has all the power in the world, but He can't use it. Or maybe He decided that He *won't* use it. Either way, He's just gotta sit there and watch all the stupid stuff we do.

I usually don't think about God when I'm watching TV or eating. It happens mostly when I'm alone in my bed, with the lights out and the crickets making noise outside my window. It also happens a lot when I have a fever and all the regular stuff I think about disappears.

When I look up at the wall again, I see some birds' nests and a million pieces of paper with people's prayers in them, all stuffed into the cracks between the stones. Everyone who comes here wants God's attention. I'll bet He loves all the notes.

They probably make Him feel like someone cares about all the cool stuff He does.

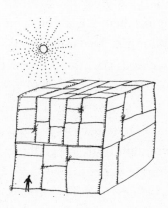

THE BATTLE OF THE TWO SOULS

I was fifteen years old when I discovered I had two distinct souls, an animal soul and a godly soul. Although I didn't have names for them then, I sensed they were there. I had a girlfriend named Ricki. I was as in love with her as a boy my age could possibly be. She broke up with me one night, and my heart shattered. I was so sick with despair that for a brief time I began to think that no longer being alive was an option worthy of my consideration.

Because time moved so slowly when I was fifteen, a hand-ful of weeks was all it took to get past the worst of the hurt, then to see with the utmost clarity how fiercely my two souls were struggling inside me. Each of them pressing for control of my body and mind. The animal soul—the one that needs sex, the one that needs attention, the one that gets angry when it doesn't get its way, the one that had me contemplating end-ing my own life—always seemed to have the upper hand. However, it did—over many years, and through much wise and gentle persuasion from my godly soul—fire its guns less often, if not end the war entirely. Once I became aware of the battle that was being waged, I could never *not* feel it.

Now, so many years later, I can still sense the two souls' furious engagement. Whether I'm making soup, playing with my grandsons, writing a song, or just putting on my shoes, I can tell they're still going at it.

It's frustrating to conclude that there will never be a decisive victory. But despite the constancy of the fight, there is hope in knowing, at the very least, that my godly soul has never given in to surrender.

LAST THOUGHTS
(NOTE TO SELF)

At the end of the road, you won't be thinking of

awards	guitars
stocks	first-class tickets
bonds	kung pao chicken
swimming pools	six-pack abs
slights	orgasms
sofas	liquor
silverware	pay raises
compliments	pay cuts
careers	notoriety
cars	weather

taxes	punctuality
hair	diamonds
weight gain	achievement
weight loss	applause
social media	politics
politics	race
winning	or revenge.
losing	

You will think about the people you have loved and the ways their love made you feel.

STARLINGS

I was in Rome at a time in my life when I was so preoccupied by all the mundane things I'd been doing to make a living that I was unmoved by the Colosseum, the Sistine Chapel ceiling, and the *Pietà*. I walked through Saint Peter's Basilica, mostly staring down at my watch, wondering when it would be time for lunch. I looked at the people around me—strangers, friends, my family members—many of them brought to tears by their nearness to these incredible human achievements. I, too, was aware of their beauty and grandeur, but there was a wall in front of me, a curtain that prevented me from feeling any of the emotions one is supposed to feel in Rome. *What's wrong with me?* I thought. *Why am I still focused on the busywork waiting for me halfway around the globe?*

It's lonely to be the one left out, the one who can't seem to join the rest of humanity in celebrating what are almost universally considered the most stirring things the world has to offer. I did a passable job of feigning enthusiasm. I did my best to gape and stand back and appear to relish these things as a cultured person, a normal person might. But what I felt was mostly emptiness.

We made our way back to the hotel, and while the others in our party were grabbing something to drink in the lobby, I went up to my room to send some emails. The curtains had been closed to keep the late afternoon sun from shining too brightly on my computer, and after twenty minutes or so, I stood up to draw them back. *I'm in Rome. What am I doing, working on nothing of any importance in this darkened hotel room?*

When I looked out the window, what I saw made me feel as though I'd lost my mind. I wondered if I hadn't accidentally swallowed a psychotropic drug with my iced tea. There was darkness, and then, suddenly, there was blinding light.

The sky was convulsing in spirals of dark gray, heaving and roiling like ink stirred by a giant spoon in a colossal glass of water. I wanted to call someone up to the room to verify what I was seeing, but there was no time. Swaths of sky kept quivering, turning. I couldn't drag myself away from the enormity of it, not even for a moment.

I thought I was dreaming. How else to explain it? The shapes were growing. Some of them were hundreds of feet high; others, seemingly thousands, careening upward, then falling with great ferocity down near the ancient rooftops. I assumed this must be what angels look like—huge, fearsome, severely gorgeous.

I saw a flock of starlings, flying in from the hills to the west, illuminated by a great shaft of amber light. I watched them join the shapes, saw them rise and fall with them, and then, with impeccable grace, become lost within them.

PEOPLE, POWER, PRAYER

Our week-old grandson is in the emergency room with my daughter and her husband, waiting to be admitted to the NICU. Although it seems imminent that he'll have to undergo open-heart surgery, I have another scenario in mind. I'm going to choose my words carefully. I'll say it's possible that the baby will not have to undergo heart surgery—better yet, I'll say he won't need any surgery at all.

I believe the words we use have a profound effect on outcomes. I began to think this way years ago after reading a story about the legendary mystic the Baal Shem Tov (which means "master of the good name"). At one time, a student of the Baal Shem Tov was heard shouting in anger at a fellow student, "I'm going to kill you!"

Alarmed, the Baal Shem Tov gathered his students together in a circle and told them to hold hands. "Behold the power of words," he said. In an instant, they fell into a hypnagogic hallucination, a kind of waking dream. Suddenly, the body of the student who'd been threatened appeared before them, his skull broken open. In the hands of the student who'd threatened him was a heavy cane, covered in blood. "Oh, Heavenly Father," the student cried. "What have I done? What have I done!"

The Baal Shem Tov clapped his hands three times, in reference to thought, speech, and action, the three ways human beings interact within the physical world. The students came to, trembling, tears of awe streaming down their faces. "What you have seen," the Baal Shem Tov said, "is that every word we speak has consequences. And while the manifestations of our words are not always apparent, they play out nonetheless, in other worlds and on other planes of reality."

I've been writing to several friends this morning, requesting their prayers for our grandson. One drove for an hour in the middle of the night to place a letter he'd composed at the grave site of a holy man. Another got his entire congregation to recite Psalms in supplication for the boy's full and speedy recovery. A third person, a colonel and a Green Beret who'd done several tours of duty in Afghanistan, sent me the following text: "I'll get the whole clan on what my mom calls the special prayer!"

The celebrated poet and recording artist Patti Smith once wrote a song called "People Have the Power." I'm not sure whom or what she had in mind when she wrote it, but the idea that people do indeed have power feels true. And now, after I've read the many emails and texts I've received, my mood has undergone a tremendous elevation. The change is palpable. The way I feel about a group of people using the power of prayer to help others is a lot like the way I view the universe at large—that we are, that everything is, intimately interconnected.

I wait for the phone to ring. I wait with a very particular intention. I wait with an awareness—an awareness without facts—that by a divine language, a divine wisdom, and a divine love the world is being re-created at this very moment. I breathe slowly, easily. Everything that's happening, even in this challenging sliver of time, is for the good.

I don't have any explanation for what occurred between this morning and now. I can't say whether my prayers or the prayers of so many others have had any effect. But one thing feels certain, at least to me: God has pulled back the curtain and let some light shine through the gloaming. This morning a team of pediatric specialists agreed that open-heart surgery on our newborn grandson would be necessary. But by 3:00 p.m., the surgery was called off.

Amen selah.

WE SEE THE BIRD

Nothing special happened this morning, at least not any-thing I can easily point to. I was standing in front of the mirror putting toothpaste on my toothbrush. But for a second, maybe less, I had the stark and sudden realization that I was alive. And that at some point I will no longer be alive. There was no intellectualizing—no *Wow, you're squeezing out toothpaste: Isn't that magical?*

It was more like I'd seen a strange bird fly by. When a strange bird flies by, we don't achieve any sort of insight. We see the bird, and then it vanishes. We retain a certain feeling, but we have no control over the bird. All day I couldn't stop thinking that one thought.

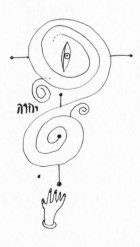

EVERYTHING
(NOTE TO SELF)

The night sky is a deep maroon. As you look up, a kind of sorrowful reverence overtakes you. You think about your mother in the cool of the night air. You remember that when you were a child she would hold you on her lap and sing, "You are my sunshine, my only sunshine…" How you felt then, nestled there, seems to you now like the purity of love. You wonder how it was that you, a person who rarely feels appreciated, could once have been the center of another human being's world, the locus of someone's gratitude for life.

The shock of recalling this feeling leaves you both melancholy and uplifted. *Where have my days gone? Where am I? Who have I become?* Two nighthawks burst from the spruce trees and lead your attention upward again, toward the dark sky.

Your mother is old, and your father is gone. Your friends are too busy to be concerned. You have a wife and children, but your time is divided between caring for them and dreaming about being someplace else. And all at once, on this singular night, the indefinable non-thing you have so desperately craved has escaped its prison and, if only for an instant, allowed you to embrace it. For now, for just this moment, you are full and steady.

The cry of the nighthawks penetrates you. They tell you that what you've been yearning for is within you now—that it has always been there. Everything. The security, the warmth, the tenderness, the very things you had tortured yourself into believing you had outgrown. You are an adult, after all, and you hadn't thought an adult was allowed to think such things, to feel such things, to need in this way. But all this is no longer true.

What you have suddenly come to realize is that you are neither fully grown nor a child—neither are you a dilettante or a master, a dullard or a genius, a tycoon or a pauper, a saint or a scoundrel, a success or an embarrassment, a mortal or a spirit—you are none of these.

The outlines of your body have vanished, just as the outlines of your awareness have vanished. You are as limitless as the whole of the sky. A wind blows in from the north, and as the night air cools further, a new thought arises. A revelation, you think. Uncomplicated and all-consuming.

I am a spirit, an extension of God, a wave of light, trapped beneath a trillion or more temporal layers, awaiting nothing more than to stand here—to stand here and watch as the clouds glide by in perfect time with the moon.

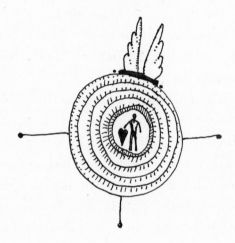

THE SPACESHIP

Picture someone who makes your skin crawl. Someone whose values you find abhorrent, someone you utterly despise. Now imagine you've been living in outer space, completely isolated from all human contact. You check the timer that's mounted on the wall of your pod. It says you've been alone in there for twenty-three years, eight months, fifteen days, five hours, and thirty-seven minutes. You look out the window of your capsule and resign yourself to the pain of not seeing another human being again for as long as you live.

And then suddenly, from out of the hollow darkness, a spaceship approaches. The ship locks onto yours, and a stranger enters the portal. Even though it's been almost a quarter of a century, when he removes his helmet you recognize him instantly. It's *him*, the person you despise.

You wrestle with your feelings. You're conflicted. But the longing for connection with another person takes precedence. You walk slowly toward him; he walks toward you. You embrace each other, both of you refusing to let go.

"Do you remember the taste of apples?" you ask without thinking.

Yes," he says. "I can still taste them, but I haven't had one in so long."

"And do you remember the smell of rain?"

He nods and says, "I do, although rain is a distant dream to me now."

There is a collision of emotions, feelings neither of you believed you'd ever experience again. You both laugh for the first time in many years.

"Do you ever close your eyes and imagine you're looking up at the blue dome of earth's sky?" he asks you.

"Every artificial morning," you answer.

You both stand in silence, without words to describe the joy.

HOW MUCH?

How much can I give?

If I'm doing the giving—that is, "I" in the physical sense, as opposed to "I" in the spiritual sense—then there's a limit. There's a limit to how much my body can lift or push or carry or press and stretch. But there's also a limit to how much giving my emotions will allow. When will I stop feeling like I'm being charitable and start feeling like I'm being taken advantage of or even abused? The emotional tiredness comes quickly for me, long before my body becomes tired. But there have been times—precious few, I'm afraid—when I've experienced a seemingly endless supply of stamina. At these times, my energy seems to come from outside myself, as if from an infinite wellspring.

I have a close friend who went through an extremely difficult period in his marriage. He was doing everything in his power to prevent a divorce. But what he wanted from me was more than advice: he was looking for hope. The most helpful thing I could do for him was to find hope within myself and then share my sense of hopefulness with him. It was my love for my friend and my empathy for his challenges that gave me the will to uncover hope and to successfully reflect it back to him. It's love, in other words, that provides the strength to raise up another human being.

Where love is present, it's possible, to the most infinitesimal of infinitesimal degrees, to receive a glimmer of God's tireless, ceaseless, and merciful capacity to give.

A STRONGLY HELD BELIEF
(NOTE TO SELF)

When your beloved's joys, sorrows, needs, and wants start to become your own, you can be certain that you've accomplished something important with your time on earth.

JOB DESCRIPTIONS

The mother offers warmth
The father shines his light
The wind sifts through the clouds
The falcons take to flight
The mason builds the home
The doctor cures the ill
The wolf howls out her song
The soldier takes the hill
The pilgrim seeks the light
The farmer sows the seed
The teacher wakes the mind
The runner longs for speed
The sky compels the ground
The school bell boldly rings
The desert waits for rain
The hawk extends its wings
The singer stirs the soul
The mourner shovels clay
The highway rounds the bend
The hand wipes tears away
The writer half reveals
The hunter makes things die
The seamstress mends the tear
The sea reflects the sky

The child absorbs the world
The victor longs for praise
The rock displays its will
The wicked waste their days
The dead recall their lives
The friendless fight despair
God is One and only
The lovers float on air

ADJUSTMENTS

A woman I love once asked me how I could have faith in God when we live in a world as frightening and uncertain as ours—a world where evil shows its face every day. It's both a good question and an impossible one to answer. Because she was in great pain, my best response was to hold her. To hear her. To be with her, without words, without explanations.

I think back on that encounter from time to time, and with no one looking to me for answers, I, too, will raise questions about my own faith in a world that is indeed full of fear and uncertainty. Those questions are also unanswerable.

Even now, God is in some sense responsible for my fingers tapping out these sentences on the keyboard of my computer, for each of the raindrops falling on the rooftops outside my window, and for every feather of every pigeon seeking shelter under the eaves. Even the so-called normal things are impossible to answer for.

The question of faith in God comes down to more practical matters: How do I cope with the not-knowing that surrounds me at every moment? How do I reconcile myself to the fact that I will never understand many of the things I take as a given—air, for example, or light, or water, or the ability to communicate my thoughts, or to give life to a child who can give birth to a child of her own? Where do I file my uncertainty about everything I experience? How can I accustom myself to the nearly supernatural phenomenon of my own consciousness? Or do I just ignore the fact that my existence and the existence of the entire universe is a miracle?

Faith is difficult. It isn't about belief; it's about adjusting to being human.

99.9 TO 0.1
(NOTE TO SELF)

You've awakened this morning, as you normally do, with the following ratio in your mind: 99.9 to 0.1. You are 99.9 percent physical, 0.1 percent spiritual.

You can feel the 99.9 without even trying: you need to pee; you need to stretch your limbs. You're hungry; your head aches; your mind is racing with worries about the future, with remorse for things you haven't achieved, with recrimination toward people who have offended you. Your heart is beating. You're breathing; you're sweating. You're also in desperate need of a shower and a cup of strong tea.

The other part, the 0.1, is there, too, but it's mostly silent, waiting for you to take notice. While 99.9 is a raging bonfire, 0.1 is an ember, barely glowing.

You've noticed that 99.9 works perfectly well all on its own. On the other hand, 0.1 is a newborn, a thing that needs to be nursed and tended to at all hours of the day. Whereas 99.9 is certain, 0.1 is vague.

As you've matured, you've found—just as you've found in the music you write and in the relationships you've fostered over the years—that the development of your spiritual side has become much more important to you than it once was. And you think, *But how do I pay attention to sensations that rarely announce themselves? How do I develop a desire to determine what is necessary and what isn't?*

As a young man, you almost always followed the urgings of 99.9. Its impulses were strong enough to make you ache. They were a roar from a volcano. Although you sensed it was there, it took many years before you began to take serious notice of the nearly silent voice of 0.1. The thing that made you most attentive to 0.1 was getting married and having children. It was through countless incidences of compromise, conciliation, and care that you began to tame 99.9—or, rather, *persuade* it, with intelligence, truth, and some kindness, to join forces with 0.1, to lend its great strength to the advancement of 0.1. That's really the goal, the ultimate prize.

There's no fighting 99.9; it's too powerful and too smart. It must come to recognize on its own that there's an advantage to being part of something it once believed was out to destroy it. It must discover the delights of 0.1, which lie beyond what it's always been seeking. That formation of an alliance between 99.9 and 0.1 takes a long time. It's infinitely more challenging than, say, becoming a professional cellist or learning to speak conversational Xhosa.

From the moment your first child, Isaac, was born, you changed in a fundamental way. The beautiful, fearsome realization that you were responsible for another human life washed over you like a twelve-foot wave. It felt as if you were seeing a new color or hearing a note that had never before been played—try to imagine the sound of an H-sharp! *This is happening, Peter. This is real; the momentous task of fatherhood is upon you.* Even 99.9 seemed to have taken notice of the change, and it started, little by little, to soften its position.

As you became more responsible, it got easier to see beyond the tangle of thoughts and impulses that 99.9 wove through your mind and body. It got easier to find subtle feelings—those that perhaps convey something of the essence of God, which you believe is to create, to love, to nurture, to develop, and to bestow.

There probably won't ever be a raging bonfire in 0.1, at least not for you. You'll need to continually search for it, direct your attention toward it, and invigorate it. But for now, at least, this is the way things are, and you've dutifully, if not always easily, accepted the challenge.

THE BIG CANVAS

I'm not sure what it is, but for the last several weeks—or has it been months?—I've been charged with a kind of electricity. I wake up each morning with all sorts of ideas, things that need to be done, things I feel almost desperate to accomplish. There are so many that if I don't write them down, I'm sure I'll forget most of them. Even now, I'm sitting here writing, pouring out my thoughts, perhaps without the requisite concern over whether anyone will care. It's as if I'm trying to convey something, purvey some essential idea before the curtain of the day falls down on me.

I remember feeling the same way around the time my dad was in a life-and-death struggle with lymphoma. I was made hyperconscious then, ineluctably aware that time was running out, that I needed to prove something, to complete something that might, in some way, slow things down. In retrospect, I can see that I was attempting to slow down the inevitable fact of his death.

Maybe that's what compels me today: an urge to slow things down, to cherish and to utilize every moment to its fullest, knowing that even if one is blessed to live to a ripe old age, mortality is out there waiting, lurking. You may think this kind of talk is morbid. I think it's actually the opposite. Seeing the end—and God willing, may the end be a long way off!—is a way of seeing the present, seeing exactly where you stand in the midst of everything else.

What I've recently come to cherish is the big canvas. We get one every day. We get to paint whatever we like. We can use it to paint love or anger. We can use it to paint hope or helplessness, fear or resolve. As we become more fully aware of the big canvas, we won't be able to ignore it. We will no longer be able to suppose, as I so often do, that our time here is without limit. We will feel, more often than we had before, the weight, the breadth, and the depth of that essential gift. After all, everything we experience is painted within each of its vast frames.

THE LEAST AMONG US

Anger is how the least among us express their sorrow. It's nothing more than a mask of protection for a small and vulnerable self. I've tried it. It doesn't work. I've heard people say that anger turns us into beasts. That's not exactly right. It reveals to the world that we are carrying so much pain that we no longer have the will to uncover the part of us that longs to love and—perhaps even more urgently—receive love.

SAGA OF THE MIRACULOUS TALKING BEAR

Somewhere around 1983, about a year before my dad died, I received a call from a woman named Ruth asking if I'd be willing to write some songs for a therapeutic teddy bear she'd dreamed up called Spinoza Bear. I was introduced to Ruth through Steven Greenberg, a friend of mine from Minneapolis who'd recently hit pay dirt as the composer and producer of the megahit "Funkytown." Ruth, a bona fide subversive by nature, named her ursine brainchild after Baruch Spinoza, the heretical seventeenth-century Sephardic Jewish philosopher.

Ruth was New Age before such a thing became commonplace. Last I heard, she was living among native tribespeople in northern British Columbia and had changed her name to Rachel Owa. I don't know this for a fact, but I can imagine that with her brilliant imagination and zeal for life, she is always the first to enter the sweat lodge, the first to ingest each season's ceremonial peyote, and the first to have exultant visions of flocks of crimson crows in some light-filled astral realm.

Back when she was still Ruth, she commissioned me to write several songs that would play on a battery-operated tape deck that fit into a zippered pouch beneath the soft brown fur of Spinoza Bear's stomach. A red heart-shaped knob on his chest served as the on-off switch. By today's standards, the technology seems crude, but at the time, with just a modicum of suspension of disbelief, it was possible to feel that the voice of the bear and the music were issuing directly from his cheery muzzle. After some deliberation, it was decided that not only would I write and sing the songs, I would also voice the kind, concerned sentiments of the bear itself.

Each of the dozen or so cassette tapes that were eventually recorded contained messages of self-empowerment, a kind of you-can-make-it-if-you-try set of affirmations. After just two years, the bear became a huge success, not as some plebeian stuffed animal but as something greater. Spinoza Bear soon found his way into hospitals, health clinics, and centers for healing of all kinds. By holding the bear and listening closely to his stories and songs of wellness and inner light, rape victims, grief-stricken parents, bone-lonely pensioners, autistic kids, and children on cancer wards across America found it possible to relieve some of their pain and fear. Aside from good karma, the bear provided me with the twenty grand in seed money that our New Wave rock band, Sussman Lawrence, used to set sail for New York City in search of fame and fortune in the spring of 1985.

❑ ❑ ❑

We were five aspiring musicians in an Oldsmobile Vista Cruiser station wagon and two roadies leading the way in a brand-spanking-new Dodge cube van. Only days after we reached the East Coast, the van, which was parked on an East Village side street, had been christened from bumper to bumper with graffiti sometime during our forty-five-minute debut set at CBGB, the renowned East Village punk-rock club.

Given the high cost of living in New York City, settling in New Jersey seemed like the thing to do. But as it turned out, there were very few homeowners interested in renting a house to a rock-and-roll band. As always, necessity demanded that I be resourceful. I hatched a plan that involved my calling on a middle-aged real estate agent named Carol. When I got her on the line, I explained that we were five medical students enrolled that fall at nearby Rutgers University in need of a quiet place to live and study.

The following morning, as the rest of the guys waited outside in the Oldsmobile, my cousin Jeff and I showed up at Carol's office in suits and ties we'd purchased at a local thrift shop. I had boned up on some medical terms—orthopedic surgical techniques, mostly—in case she needed proof that we were actually medical students. But there had been no need. We had the cash and seemed honest enough—"honest" enough, at least, to let her know that a few of us were also part-time musicians and that there might be some music playing—quietly, of course—from time to time, just to ease the strain of our intense studies.

Two days later, Jeff and I woke up early, signed the lease papers, and pulled our now multihued, invective-laden cube van into the driveway of 133 Busteed Drive in Midland Park, New Jersey.

Trying for as much discretion as possible, lest the neighbors notice anything out of the ordinary, we backed the van up to the garage, then lugged the gear up a short flight of stairs and into a large, unfurnished living room. Once upstairs, we began unloading beer-stained amplifiers, at least a dozen guitar cases, a drum set packed tightly into three large metal flight cases, assorted keyboards, and an entire PA system and lighting rig. Aside from some scrapes in the hardwood floor and a gaping hole or two in the walls, the load-in was speedy and efficient. We were up and practicing by late afternoon, our New Wave rock music blaring fast and loud into the New Jersey autumn night. It was nothing short of a miracle that we ever received a single complaint from our neighbors.

A few months after we had settled into the squalor of our band-house commune (we named it Busteed Manor), Ruth called me at dinnertime, long distance. I took the receiver as far out of the kitchen as the pigtail cord would allow so I could hear her over the din of our turkey ham, boiled white rice, and Progresso chicken soup supper.

After some catching up, Ruth gently let me know me that some psychic friends of hers had told her I had just a few months left on the planet.

"What? Those freaks told you I was gonna die?"

Ruth was practiced at this kind of thing, it seemed, although her nonchalance about my imminent demise didn't make me feel any less concerned. "They asked me to find out if you'd like to come in for a free consultation," she said. I needed to be in Minneapolis for some shows anyway, so I figured I'd go and experience what a psychic consultation was like. In fact, I truly *needed* help then—any sort of help. Yes, I was now on the East Coast with my band, living out a long-held dream. But the excitement of leaving home also brought with it a strange and troubling sensation. It was as if I were looking up at the sky, waiting for a boulder to fall and crush my bones.

❑ ❑ ❑

The following week, in Minneapolis, on the morning of my appointment with the psychics, I found my mother, who was normally quite composed, flitting around her kitchen, humming quietly to herself. She had agreed to a lunch date that afternoon with the contrabass player from the Minnesota Orchestra. It was her first date since she had married my dad, at the age of eighteen—and her first date since he died.

"Does this blouse look good on me?" she asked. "Be honest."

"Yeah, it looks great," I said.

Truthfully, I was uncomfortable watching my mother dart around the house like a schoolgirl, primping for a date with some dude who wasn't my dad. Yes, it'd been two years since he died, and given all that she'd been through, it wasn't like she didn't deserve to live a little. After all, I thought, it's just lunch. But the more I saw of this weird, giddy side of her, the less I liked it.

A car honked. It was Ruth.

❑ ❑ ❑

Twenty minutes later, Ruth and I parked near a long row of newly built town houses in Brooklyn Center, a northern suburb of Minneapolis. The door to one of them opened, and we were greeted by a man and woman in their mid-forties, both smiling in a sort of off-putting way.

The couple led us up a small flight of carpeted stairs and into a dimly lit living room. The two sat facing each other in matching wooden rockers as Ruth disappeared into the kitchen and I settled nervously into a faux-leather armchair. The couple appeared to be a husband-and-wife psychic tag team, and they rushed headlong into the consultation by asking me if I'd like to give them some names of people I knew. "We'll be able to tell you all about them," the woman said. I guessed it was just some flashy method of showing off their psychic abilities. "The first names are enough," said the man.

My cousin Jeff—the keyboardist in Sussman Lawrence and my partner in "medical school" crime—is a true musical genius, a pianist of remarkable facility. He's also had to contend with neuromuscular tics most of his life. In fact, Jeff and I had given them names. When his thumbs bent spasmodically downward, for example, we called it the Southerner. When his palms flexed upward in a sort of hand-waving motion, we called it the Reckless Greeter. With his eyebrows pinched together, his lips compressed, and his eyes blinking uncontrollably, he looked like someone who was very curious about his environment. We called that one Curious Man. Jeff's most frequent tic was also his most unsettling. We called that one Round the World. It involved his eyeballs rolling wildly around in their sockets.

I figured I'd start the game with him. "Okay, let's go with Jeff," I said.

Suddenly, to my astonishment, the corners of both psychics' mouths formed narrow half smiles. Their eyebrows began squeezing together; their eyes were blinking—open, shut, open, shut—perfectly mimicking Jeff's Curious Man. Then: "The music—he can't stop the music!" the woman shouted in excitement. Her husband, whose hands began an uncannily accurate imitation of the Reckless Greeter, added, "Yes, good God, the music! Can't you feel it just pouring out of him?"

I was thinking this had to be some kind of brilliant trick, albeit a devilish one. It was astounding, yes, but I wasn't yet convinced that the psychics were for real. So then I said the name Beverly, my mother's, and they both giggled. It's disconcerting to see adults giggle at any time, but when a pair of middle-aged psychics giggles at the mention of your bereaved mother's name, well, it's triply so.

"She's doing something she feels guilty about," the woman offered.

"Yes," said the man. "Something she's afraid of doing, but it seems to us that she's also very excited."

Almost in unison, the psychics said, "She's acting like a little schoolgirl today!"

How could they have known what I'd experienced myself for the first time in my life that very morning? I hadn't told anyone at that point. If these two freaks had wanted my undivided attention, they had it then.

The room fell silent. I didn't dare speak. They had officially scared the living crap out of me. Then they broached the subject I'd come all that way to talk about.

"Is it your wish to leave the planet?" the woman asked, more casually than I liked.

I paused and breathed deeply. It was a question I thought about longer than a mentally stable person might have.

"No," I finally told them. "I have no intention of leaving anytime soon."

This seemed to relieve them. The man took over. "The reason we've been so concerned about you is that we believe music is more important to you than you may be aware. It forms your very essence, and by working as single-mindedly as you have to get a record deal, and by making the kind of pop music you've been making with your band, you've been cheapening and compromising your integrity. You've been, in a sense, unfaithful to your muse. That's what's causing this spiritual disconnect, and should it continue, my wife and I both feel it will shorten your stay here."

His wife took over. "What you need to do is uncover a deeper, more honest expression in your music, something closer to the bone. We know you love the blues and reggae. We think it'll be helpful to start playing music you love rather than music you think will sell."

By that time, tears were spilling down my cheeks. "There's this song," I stammered, "that I wrote for my dad more than two years ago, on his last Father's Day, a song that almost no one has heard. It's something that was written with the sole intention of connecting with him before he died. It's on a cassette tape, just sitting there on a shelf in my closet."

"Why not put that song out as your next single?" the man said.

I was suddenly speechless. Why had I never thought of that? It was such a simple yet profound idea. I flew back to New Jersey determined to release not just the one song but also an entire album dedicated to my dad.

◻ ◻ ◻

The guys in the band picked me up in our Oldsmobile wagon at the Newark airport the next day. We were standing around the luggage carousel waiting for my bags when I told them I was going to record a solo record, a tribute to my father, whom they all loved and respected. My bandmates understood that this was something I needed to do. They also knew it wasn't just talk. A solo album, produced for whatever reasons, also signaled the possibility that the one-for-all-and-all-for-one ethos of the band may well have been coming to end. Nevertheless, the guys played their hearts out on the record, and by doing so they tacitly gave me their blessings and assurances that whatever happened with it would be for the best. The recording featured the song I'd written for my dad, and it eventually became my debut album, *This Father's Day*, for Island Records.

Its release was a powerful catalyst for me. It took me from the place where I had been, locked up in pain and confusion, to some other, hopeful place. Even before my meeting with the psychics, I thought I'd gotten past most of the hurt and that it was simply time to grit my teeth and persevere. But I was mistaken. The process of mending torn hearts is never as pat as that. As much as I needed to forget, to emerge clear-eyed from the jumble and rawness of my father's death, I knew I'd have to face my worst fears repeatedly in the years to come. But I felt ready. I also knew, in a way I hadn't before, that I really didn't want to die.

□ □ □

I realize now that my father is with me in whatever way it is that spirits move with people they love and leave behind. I also understand that he was proud of me then and that somehow he is proud of me still. In many ways his death, painful as it was, presented me with a bridge over which I could traverse some of the petty concerns I might have otherwise gotten wrapped up in as a young man.

While he was suffering during his last four years of life, I found myself in a different state of mind from that of my bandmates, who, despite their own challenges, were for the most part blithely moving through their young lives. I'm not saying that pain made me wise: it's just that pain can, for people willing to accept its hard lessons, provide a bit of perspective—shine some light on what's sacred and what's not. During those years, in my early twenties, I was working very hard to become famous, whatever that might have meant. I felt that I needed to reach some level of achievement before my dad died. I suppose I was conducting a search for miracles.

It's no wonder. For my family—and for me, at least—miracles seemed to have been in very short supply back then.

It's miracles, after all, that propel us forward, that encourage us to move with some degree of willingness into the next day. But despite what we might believe, it's hardly ever the big miracles that truly move us. The seas can part; we can win the lottery; we can even become rock stars—and still, those phenomenal circumstances are never what matter most. In the end, the only miracle worth wishing for is to recognize the smallest splendors, the most inconsequential truths, and the overlooked rhythms that connect us to the people we love.

WINDOW CLEANER
(NOTE TO SELF)

Change is the perfect window cleaner. It scours the filth from your perceptions of the world. It helps you see what you've always known but somehow always forget: that change isn't a string of problems to be solved or a list of burdens to be borne.

Change cries out, roars, and sings. Change has the power to take you back to your beginning, to take you back to when life was a spiral of ever-evolving beauty. And when you rediscover that misplaced part of yourself, you begin to see beauty in all its forms—in sadness, in joy, in loss, in discovery, in uncertainly, in hope, in love, in fear, in triumph, in failure—in falling down and in rising up.

If you want to keep your windows clean, keep asking yourself these questions:

Who do you love?
Who do you trust?
What do you need?
Who can you heal?
What gives you joy?
What brings you hope?
What conveys meaning?
What are your aspirations?
What can you give?
What do you consider sacred?
What would you give your life for?

MORNING

The older I get, the greater the number of people who become beloved to me. How can I not rise early and pray for them?

BEING HUMAN

Animal urges
Angelic tenderness
Screaming rage
Compassionate embraces
Hateful glances
Warm invitations
Spite-filled lies
Resolute truths
Myopic prejudice
Unconditional acceptance
Hopeless thoughts
Towering prayers
Vengeful plans
Benevolent aspirations
Cold austerity
Gentle warmth
Perverse justice
Healing mercy
Petty jealousy
Sympathetic generosity
Cowering weakness
Unwavering courage

5 PERCENT WORDS

When I started to speak again after a total of six weeks of vocal rest, before and after surgery to remove a benign nodule from my left vocal cord, my voice was weak, and only gradually was I regaining confidence in it. But more pressing than the technical question of regaining my voice was how I decided to use it from that point on.

It's human nature to love something most just as it slips away. One almost never delves into the meaning of a thing, the essence of a thing, until it's removed from one's life. The more sudden the loss, the more deeply felt it is. A good friend once playfully derided my use of words as a kind of fortress—a "fortress of words," she called it—something I would routinely defend myself with. I hated to admit it, but I knew she was right. There had been something frightening about being cast into the world without words, my longtime protectors. But there was something wonderful about it as well, something liberating about shedding my armor and experiencing the vulnerability that came in its wake.

My first words after those six weeks were nothing astonishing, I assure you. "Can I please get some tea and honey?" "I need to schedule another appointment." "Which way to the elevator?" But after having had some time to consider what my next sentences would be, I found myself wondering, *What is it that I stand for? And how will my words make a powerful case for those ideals?*

In not speaking, one tends to hear a lot more of the conversations of other people. You hear a lot about the things they desire and how they use their words to obtain those things. If I had to do a rough analysis of the things people say, I'd argue that 50 percent of all words are purely procedural, as in: "Please pass the olive oil." Another 25 percent are no more than sounds to fill uncomfortable silences: "Hey, kid, how's school going?" (In my experience, that is the sentence—in any language known to mankind—that is least likely to get a child to respond.) Then, I'm sad to say, I'd have to ascribe 20 percent to what I call damning words. Words such as: "Did you see how fat Phillip's gotten?" We love our damning words because we can barely keep ourselves from making the illogical assumption that if someone else is doing poorly, we must be doing well.

And then I'd leave only around 5 percent for the best words—by my count, the most underused words of all. Here, by way of example, I'll offer two truthful sentences to the people I love most in the world, people who have stood by me and taught me how beautiful it is to feel connected.

Your friendship and love are the most meaningful things in the world to me. In this moment, I am thinking of you, and I cherish the blessing of our bond more than you know.

FIRST THINGS FIRST

As soon as I open my eyes in the morning, I say an age-old prayer of thanks called the *Modeh Ani*. And though it consists of just one sentence, the timing is critical—especially on cold, dark mornings. According to tradition, it's said immediately upon waking so that gratitude floods our very first thoughts: "I give thanks to you, Living and Eternal King, for you have returned my soul to me with compassion; your truth is great."

Like so many routines and behaviors that purport to improve one's life, waking up and intoning a two-thousand-year-old prayer is far easier to think about than to do. I found my own attempts more often a garbled grunt than a consequential invocation. But one morning, I ignored my native sloth, skepticism, and general tendency toward melancholy and did something different after mumbling the prayer. I sat up in bed and began to voice those things I felt grateful for. By doing so, I saw the intricate details of my surroundings as I rarely had—not as unimportant, taken-for-granted minutiae but as very real, and very important, contributions to my well-being and my ability to turn my creative ideas into reality. After reciting the Modeh Ani, I stared up at the shadows on the A-frame ceiling in our bedroom and said the following words, quietly but nonetheless out loud: "I am thankful I woke up in a space with a roof that protects me from the rain."

The idea of protection from rain is so basic that I often forget how many people in the world lack this luxury. And though our bedroom is nice, until that moment I never would have used the word "luxurious" to characterize anything about it. But as I watched the gathering clouds from my window and rain seemed ever more imminent, the term seemed increasingly apt.

Then I moved my concentration to the bed: "I am thankful for these blankets; they're so soft and warm." From there I looked at my hands: "I am profoundly grateful that I can move my fingers at will, grateful that I can use them to write, draw, and play guitar." A stream of blessings then flooded my mind: the hot running water in the bathroom (another underappreciated luxury); my close friends (I said the names of at least ten of them aloud); my mother and my siblings; the vivid memories of my late father and sister; finally, my wife Maria, our four children, and our grandchildren. Gradually I shifted from a blasé mood into something far different: I experienced the dramatic mental shift from "I need more" to "I have so much."

EXPANSIONS

One evening in late November of 1989, Maria and I were eating hummus and grilled schnitzel at an Israeli restaurant on Beverly Drive in Los Angeles. Maria was pregnant with our first child, but it seemed as if everyone there was smoking, and we were worried about the baby; the due date was just another couple of days away. We headed home and went to bed early.

At 3:00 a.m., Maria woke me. "I feel contractions," she said. "Let's get our clothes on." And we did, but since it was so cold, we got back under the covers. The contractions continued throughout the darkness of the predawn hours, and at seven sharp we left for the hospital.

In the labor and delivery room I overheard the nurse and sensed her growing anxiety. "The baby is breech," she said in her calmest voice. Maria was rushed into the surgery ward, where I was instructed to put on scrubs and a mask. I did as I was told. I sat and prayed for a perfect outcome and read from the book of Psalms. A short time later our birthing coach was able to turn the baby around. And then, without any drugs or surgery, Maria gave birth to a healthy baby boy.

I was surprised when he came out. Surprised by the fact that he was so human. So fully formed. How is it, I thought, that I've never felt this kind of love for anything or anyone?

How can I explain any of what I was feeling at that moment so many years ago except to say that an entirely new set of emotions had been unearthed? Now our son was born. I felt emotions let loose from everywhere. From music, from love, from sky, from family, from food, from soil, from sea; from the word of God to the words of children—all of it told me that what is possible is what you believe is possible.

DIFFICULTIES
(NOTE TO SELF)

It's effortless to believe in trees, effortless to believe in the sky, your own body, the ocean. They make sense. You are a physical being; you relate easily to the physical world. But things of the spirit speak softly, tread lightly, appear faintly. It is difficult for you to believe in what is difficult to sense.

Through much trial and error, you've found it helps to embark on a process of imbuing the "normal" things in your life with a sense of astonishment, to trade the rigidity of knowing for the malleability of wonder. Like any serious practice, this, too, has been difficult. But by focusing for a few hours each day on the miraculous nature of, say, the faces of people you see on the street, the random thoughts in your mind, your ability to speak, to breathe, to read, and to understand what you're reading—anything, really—you've become estranged, little by little, not from reality but from the limited reality you had created for yourself, the one that says: *Everything is the result of a random "natural" force.*

This way, things you had previously conceived of as normal begin to reveal themselves as being miraculously and continually created—here, but at the same time existing elsewhere. That revelation has been one of the most profound experiences of your life. It has made you more open to change than you had been before. As a result, it has made you more willing to give and less eager to receive. Because your spirit is the aspect of you that most easily senses the miraculous, the more often it does so, the more prominent your spiritual nature becomes.

Following the rules and dictates of society has helped you in many ways, of course. But in other ways it's made you see the world with a kind of tunnel vision. At this point in your life, you've stopped caring so much about what other people think of you and gained some of the courage it takes to find and walk your own path. That hasn't been difficult, as you once thought it would be.

SIBLINGS

I start with these assumptions: The way you see the color green is not the way I see it. My feelings about love, about shame, about strength and weakness, fear and doubt, self-worth and humility, success and ruination, prayer and anger, morality, courage, God, hope, heat, ice, succumbing to the darkness, basking in the light—for neither of us will they ever be the same.

If we happen to meet, I will go gently with you. I will carry with me the understanding that we are both irreplaceable, both deserving of compassion. After all, haven't we been born to live out our days beneath the same sky? And even though we are strangers, shouldn't that in some way make us siblings, too?

REMINDER

I have a hand-drawn sign hung above my desk. I wrote it to remind myself each day not to get lost in things that don't matter.

> *The trouble you feel is of your own making. It lives only in your mind. Slow down; everything is all right. You have what you need. For now, you have everything you need.*

AT THE MOMENT OF THE EMERGENCE OF STARS

At the moment of the emergence of stars
When dusk has turned to night
What's fixed becomes unmoored
And day slips out of sight

Darkness engulfs the dusk
Silence overtakes the din
Dreams blot out all reason
Faith supplants all sin

At the moment of the emergence of stars
The birth of hope begins
The mind turns from the outward
To the depths of the silence within

The change is all-consuming
Proof that "now" is a lie
It flutters off like a breath
Like an echo that soars to the sky

At the moment of the emergence of stars
It seems like a lifetime has passed
How can I cope with the loss
Of the days that vanish so fast?

Inside the shadows of longing
There's a weight that can't be explained
A pang neither joyous nor grievous
A space neither narrow nor wide

It's not that we are impatient
It's not that we are unwise
It's not that we're lacking for miracles
We've just forgotten how to open our eyes

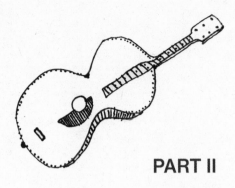

PART II

SHADOWS

Chord suggestion: D minor

*When you're writing a song, don't worry about not knowing
exactly what it is you're saying. Your feelings, especially
those that are dark or hidden, are more powerful than
your feelings about what has already been revealed.*

SUSIE

I'm in Israel with Maria and our four kids in my friend Doron's kitchen, eating fried Libyan potatoes and chicken thighs. After the meal, Maria and I head downstairs to start packing our suitcases. Our family's been in Israel for more than a month, and later this evening we're finally leaving for home. I've spent much of this trip worrying about our older son, Isaac, who suffered his first broken heart just a few days after we arrived. His girlfriend back in LA snapped it in two via instant message, and as a result, he's been even more sullen and more reluctant than usual to go with the rest of the family on our daily drives—drives that are, admittedly, often no more than directionless excursions, crisscrossing this hot and strange country in a rented van in search of something I have yet to define.

◻ ◻ ◻

I was eight years old when I made my first trip to Israel, in June of 1968, almost exactly a year after the Six-Day War. My parents had been in Italy the autumn before, and while vacationing in Rome they learned that there were inexpensive flights leaving twice a week from Rome to Tel Aviv. The whole of Israel was giddy at the time, momentarily unburdened of its insecurities by the stunning success of its victory in the war, which increased the size of the young nation by more than two-thirds.

Once in Israel, my mother finally had a use for the crumpled piece of paper she'd been carrying in her purse for the previous several months—paper on which she'd scribbled the phone numbers of distant Israeli relatives on both her father's and her mother's side, Romanians all. One woman whom my mother met for the first time on that trip and whom she was especially fond of was named Osnat. Osnat, a frail, shy woman—at least I thought so when I first met her—was technically my mother's second cousin once removed. She had the misfortune of remaining in Europe while the Nazis were on the move. I found the story of her spending five entire days hiding in the liquid filth of an outhouse and breathing through a tube when the Germans came near especially compelling.

Meeting scores of warm and loving relatives and being feted by them and referred to as their "dear American *mishpacha*" was partly why my parents were both so taken with Israel—that and the Israeli people themselves, the Sabras, so proud and brash, and the ancient beauty of the land. With some talk of perhaps making *aliyah*, or at least exploring the idea of moving to Israel, my parents, my siblings, my aunt Shelly and uncle Harold and their children—my first cousins—along with Grandma Rose and her younger brother, Uncle Sol, gathered up a month's worth of warm-weather clothing and flew en masse to Tel Aviv. We were greeted at Lod Airport by a crush of relations, all of them clamoring to hug and kiss us. And then as the sun descended into the Mediterranean and night fell over the coastal plain, they drove us all north in a ragtag caravan of tiny old Fiats, Renaults, and Peugeots to the beach town of Netanya, where we stayed for the entire summer in a small tumbledown flat just behind the house Osnat shared with her diminutive yet powerful Turkish husband, Shlomo.

❏ ❏ ❏

I continue packing my suitcase at Doron's place. After finally getting it to close, I notice three voice messages on my cell phone. I sit down to listen. The first one's from my brother-in-law Russell, in New Jersey.

Get hold of me as soon as you get this.

The next message is from him as well.

Call me as soon as possible.

The last one comes from someone at El Al airlines.

Call your family. Der is been an emergency.

Moments are elongating, stretching. I feel myself receding into individual pockets of time, each one a second or a year. I stare off at a photo on Doron's wall. It's of a young Bedouin girl with a clay jug of water balanced on her head. Time is moving slowly, and I'm thinking, *Where is this Bedouin girl going? Who needs water?* I watch the hands of an electric clock as they move in stutter step. I hear the clink of melting ice falling to the bottom of a glass that's on the table beside me.

Emergency?

My mom is getting older, but she's in good health. Maybe it's my uncle Mark. He's in his early eighties and deep into Alzheimer's.

No, it couldn't be Uncle Mark. I mean, I love the guy, but El Al airlines leaving messages?

My brother, Paul? He rides his bike to work every day even when it's raining. That would be worth a call from El Al.

I dial New Jersey. It's just after four in the morning there. My sister Nina answers. "There was an accident. An old woman fell asleep at the wheel." And then: "Susie's dead. They tried to cut her out with the Jaws of Life."

I go into zombie emergency mode. "Okay. I'll get back to ya," I say. I say this just as I might say, "I'll get back to ya about those pillows for the sofa in the living room."

Zombie emergency mode is good. It's good because I need to be calm. I need to change our flights. Good because I need to get our family to Minneapolis instead of home to LA. Good because there will be a funeral to get to, luggage to be shipped, phone calls to be made.

"What? What is it?" Maria needs to know, and so I repeat what I'd just heard. "There was an accident…" She's bracing herself against the tile floor, where she'd been sitting. I look up at the Bedouin girl with the jug on her head as I'm speaking. "It was somewhere in Wisconsin." Maria holds her breath until I say, "Susie's dead." And then she explodes into weeping like tissue paper bursting into flames. I look up at the photo of the Bedouin girl once more. There are some camels loping behind her that I hadn't noticed before.

My sister is gone. Susie, my little sister, the one who quietly distinguished herself as the only person I'd ever met who took no joy whatsoever in the most joy-filled of all human pursuits: ripping fellow human beings to shreds behind their backs. She never said a bad word about anyone; I mean this literally. Susie and I were close, close in age and close to each other, especially when our older siblings, Nina and Paul, went off into the world. When we were little, maybe four and five years old, Susie and I used to play a game called unborn duckies. I'm sure it was my name and my invention.

The game consisted of our going under the covers of our parents' bed and crawling down to the foot of it, where it was dark and hard to breathe. We'd stay there for long stretches in wordless communion. The game itself was just a pretext. Even when I was a young kid it would have been painfully embarrassing for me to be caught trying to create the kind of intimacy people must experience by being born together, like twins. Even then I needed to feel the comfort of an ironclad fealty to another human being. Now, I'm sad to say, there is just one duck.

It's hard to overstate how difficult it was to travel by taxi to Tel Aviv in a state of compartmentalized anguish and how hard it was to explain to the pretty young woman at the El Al ticket counter that I needed to change our entire family's destination from LA to Minneapolis less than eight hours before our flight was scheduled to depart because my sister had just died.

The taxi ride from Tel Aviv back to Doron's house was perfectly quiet. Because I'd numbly told him about it, the Moroccan-born driver I'd hired knew enough not to say a word, knew enough to just allow the silence to wash over us as the sun began to set in a hazy sky over the Mediterranean.

Twenty-five hours later, our family was the last to arrive in Minneapolis. Everyone's been waiting for us. Paul and I exchanged the same incredulous glances we shared the night our dad died. The kind that convey an awareness that from this moment on, every word and every action is on the verge of being either the most hilarious or the most tragic.

The crash of the juxtaposition felt like a peek behind a scrim, like an invitation into a greenroom where a universe of actors sits, adjusting their makeup, reviewing their lines. *It's not supposed to be this way. I am feeling too much. I know I'm here, but I'm not. I have one foot on earth and the other in a terribly disordered world.*

As I looked over at Maria and the kids, exhausted and gathered together with their luggage near the doorway of my mom's home, I was experiencing two overwhelming epiphanies: One, that I, like everyone assembled here, am alive. And two, that I, like everyone assembled here, am a composite of spirit and flesh. In any case, I walked down the hallway to my mom's refrigerator to see what was there for us to eat. I was hungry, so insatiably hungry.

MEA CULPA

My sister Susie, her husband Peter, and two of their kids were driving home from Camp Ramah in their Toyota minivan. It was visitors' day up in scenic Conover, Wisconsin; they'd driven up to see Michelle, Susie's oldest. I don't know what happened at the site of the accident. Here's what I conjure in my mind based on what little I was told: An elderly woman driving a Cadillac down a two-lane highway, trees on either side; the woman's eyelids slowly slipping down over tired old eyes, a dream of a firstborn son from long ago. Then an awful crash.

Susie spoke a few words to Peter and her girls from the overturned minivan before she died. Perhaps she said good-bye; I'm not sure. She was trapped in the wreckage as the rest of her family was taken away and treated at a nearby hospital. But Susie had bled too much internally before first responders could extricate her with the Jaws of Life. My brother, Paul, and my mom saw Susie covered with blood on a gurney in the hospital. She was DOA.

Somehow, I always knew Susie would be the first of my siblings to die. She was never strongly rooted in the world. You could see right through her skin. It was like the animal part of her, the very stuff of her, was too thin. It was like the shock of suddenly seeing naked flesh through a tear in a blouse—that's how easily you could see her spirit. She was incredibly strong, but she seemed vulnerable, too, as if she were too kind to be human.

By the way, if you ever unintentionally kill someone in a car accident, I suggest you study this letter her daughters received from the woman responsible for Susie's death. It's good.

> *I cannot find adequate words to express my sorrow for the loss of your mother. We lost our youngest son, Vernon, at the age of seventeen, shortly before his high school graduation, in a gun accident. I only share this with you to let you know that I have some idea of the horrible pain and loss you are going through. I wish your mother's life would have been spared and mine taken instead. I live with that anguish every day. I would never intentionally hurt anyone. I simply do not know what happened the day of the accident. I will continue to ask for God's forgiveness and ask him to watch over you and your family. I pray that only good things happen to you. I hope that someday you will find it in your heart to forgive me. I'm truly sorry for your loss and pain.*

BENEATH THE CRUST
(NOTE TO SELF)

Here on the surface, on the skin, on the crust, there can be no understanding. And yet this is where you've spent so many of your days. Only lately have you summoned the courage to go up and out—and mostly, down inside yourself. It's there that you've found things you never expected to find. It's there that you saw and felt what is so often spoken about but so seldom experienced—the knowledge that everything is wed to every other thing. An awareness that though there may be a certain man on a certain street that you have never met, you and he are indeed connected and inseparable.

You became filled with the belief that on one glorious morning not too long from now, a song will be sung, a fish will leap, a poem will be read, a beggar will receive a gift, a bird will take flight, a flower will bloom, a donkey will bray, an infant will nurse, an apple will ripen, a story will be told, a lion will roar, a dancer will dance, a child will smile, the sun will rise—and as the whole world watches, each person on the planet will say to him or herself:

> *I have been mistaken. I have remained on the surface of my own life, not because I found pleasure there but because I lacked the courage to love fully, to love the way I intuited was possible but wouldn't dare attempt. I lacked the courage to leave my place and travel beneath the skin, beneath the crust.*

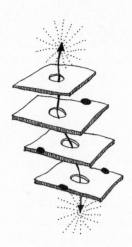

NOTHING TO SAY

At Susie's funeral, among the crowd, I see my mother's best friend, Carolyn. As I approach her, tears fill her eyes. She says nothing because she knows there is nothing to say.

Carolyn is one of the wisest people I know. Her husband, Burton, died many years ago, and immediately after his funeral—at the shivah house, to be precise—their twenty-five-year-old son, Marty, dropped dead of a brain aneurysm.

My mom got a call from Carolyn the day it happened. "Beverly," she said. "Martin died."

"No, Carolyn," my mom said with solemnity and pity. "Marty didn't die; it was Burton."

But my mom was wrong: Marty did die, on the day of his own father's funeral. Trust me—this woman Carolyn has mastered the art of moving forward when there are no more steps to take, giving comfort when there is nothing left to give, and still wrestling with faith, even when it feels like God will be forever in hiding.

VISITING

No matter how often I do so, visiting the grave site of a loved one remains a singular experience. It's a time to mourn, but also to reflect and to arrive at the visceral and humbling understanding that God runs the world—no one and nothing else.

COMPASSION

After Susie died, I was asked if I still believed in God. The question seemed somewhat absurd. The sky was still above me; the sun still shone. I was still speaking and walking on the surface of a world that God constantly brings into being. I was anguished, but how could I not still believe?

Admittedly, my prayers were full of anger. It was as if I'd turned my back on God even as I was mouthing them. And then, one morning not long after Susie's death, it occurred to me that the creator of tears, the creator of grief, must be exquisitely aware of the profundity of grief. How else can a thing become manifest if not by its creator? How could the author of anguish not know the sensation of pain? It dawned on me, too, that God's pain must be infinitely worse than my own. Had God not created my sister? Had God, whose capacity for love is infinite, not loved her more than I did?

That morning my prayers began to change. They contained an element of compassion for God.

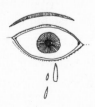

SUSPENDED BY NO STRING
(NOTE TO SELF)

You wake from a fitful sleep. It's just past 3:00 a.m., and with your last dream all but forgotten, you look up at the moon-cast patterns on the ceiling and the walls. You're thirsty. You walk downstairs. A light from a small fixture glows near the ceiling above the landing. Your head feels strange: not dizzy, just different. You wonder if you're coming down with something. You've gone downstairs for a drink of water, that's all. You felt one of the most familiar, most primitive sensations: the machine of your body telling you that you need more fluids to stay alive. Only your thirst is present.

In some way, you've become devoid of knowledge. It's not that you don't *know* things—random facts, names of people and places, makes of automobiles (Joaquin, Boston, Lincoln Continental); you haven't forgotten those. But what you now believe is that the miracle of your having been born is something you can no longer ignore.

Most mornings, you get up thinking, *Today's the day I'll win something, or make something, or meet someone, or stumble upon something so significant that it'll change everything.* But as always, the day comes, and it passes. You read the news; you make your phone calls and have your meetings. Later, you see your spouse and your children, and you feel a glimmer of something akin to love, but mostly you're tired. And at night, when you lie in bed, you're hoping that what you were looking for today you will find tomorrow. And so up until this moment at the bottom of the stairs, in a small but very real way, you've been waiting to die. No, of course not! You don't *want* to die. But you also feel that you've been waiting for this all to end.

You look up at the fan above your kitchen table and watch it spin. You are suddenly startled by your ability to see. You can scarcely process what this means, but you try. *I, the me inside me*, you think, *the I that maintains its conception of being an individuated someone, am absorbing my physical surroundings by means of these moist, gelatinous balls that fit perfectly into sockets in the front of my skull.* To no one, you say, "Why have I never noticed this?" It's not as if you haven't seen before, it's just that now, seeing—your ability to see—strikes you as a magnificent power, a miraculous faculty that went unnoticed until this very moment because it's always present. Over time, you became inured to the power of your own sight.

You move to the sink. You lift the handle on the faucet and watch as water pours out. You are struck by how beautiful and mysterious water is as it flows into the sink—beautiful enough to make you weep. Yes. You've broken down in tears, and you muffle the sounds with your hands so that no one in your house wakes up in the middle of the night thinking that some terrible thing happened that made you cry here all alone in the dark. But you're not sad, are you? Your joy is beyond the ability of words to express, and so you cry. Tears are what happen when we arrive at the very edge of language. You are there now, standing on that edge. And you cup your hands under the stream and bring the water to your lips. You drink and you ascend in joy with each swallow. You are overwhelmed by water! Drinking water seems at this moment like one of the most profound experiences you've ever had. And you wonder, *Just who is it that's experiencing all this?*

There is a window, the one over the sink. You look outside. You see mostly darkness, and the darkness itself calls to you, asks you to move into it, to enter it somehow. You walk outside. When you look up at the sky, you see the same stars you've seen since you were a child. But now, unlike every other time you've seen those stars (except when you first saw them as a child), they make you shiver with awe. *They are a thing*, you think, *so wondrous that words are not strong enough for the telling*. You walk farther out onto the grass and say out loud, as if in prayer: "I've been searching all my life for something to break the monotony, to heal me of my uncertainty, of my anxiousness, of my nagging sense that there is no purpose, no design, no miracle, no thing that's mystical or truly beautiful." But now, somehow, you've found it. And this knowledge comes without words. It is a dance that's lodged in your muscle memory—a dance that alludes to, that hints at, that points toward these truths…

The cool grass on your toes and under the soles of your feet. The sound of night birds; the swallow and the heavy great horned owl. The trilling of the crickets as they call for mates in the windless late summer air. The smell of jasmine wafting from all sides, dreamy and full. The roar of jets, tiny in the vast reaches of the sky, moving in from the ocean, laden with travelers, asleep and dreaming as they rocket home to loved ones—or to empty rooms.

Here, under the darkened firmament, you are no more and no less than what everyone on earth has always been: a naked and fragile figure, suffused with an immutable spirit, propelling yourself here and there, communicating your innermost thoughts, inclined toward both love and war, sex and prayer, spilling blood and bringing soup to the poor. And all the while breathing, as if the very act of breathing were a supplication, a plea to touch the face of God as He peers down in silent wonder at His creation. Now, with your thirst finally slaked, you have come to appreciate what you've never allowed yourself to know and may never have suspected was there to know: that being alive on this perfectly round blue planet, suspended by no string and spinning in the black void of space, is enough.

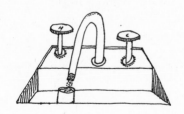

AFTERNOON PRAYER

Here at the edge of belief, at the boundary between scream and supplication, I am falling before You, begging as a child for love and for mercy. When tears come, I will be broken in a way that leaves me whole, emptied in a way that leaves me full, darkened by shadows, which I know can only be cast by light. From there I will wait for You.

I am stubborn that way; I will no longer allow myself to walk alone.

RATIONAL

There is nothing rational about insisting that the universe functions on rationality. For example, I've just woken up after having dreamed that Susie, whose death occurred twenty-five years ago, had been asleep in a hidden cellar that was three levels below the basement of our childhood home. There is little rationality about my waking from the dream with my heart pounding and my sense of loss acutely recollected. Not to mention the irrationality of the six variously colored pigeons that have suddenly alighted on the ledge of my window.

Rationality is the brush of gray paint we apply to a world whose colors are so vivid, whose dimensions are so vast, and whose essence is so far beyond our ken that without that pallid overlay we would surely lose our minds.

CIRCLES

Under a dimming sky
we watch for stars and
grow ever more uncertain.

As if the earth
that stretches before us
were created
to swallow us whole.

As if the gnarled branches
arrayed above us
hang as omens of loss.

As if each tender blade of grass
bending under our bootheels
signals an
encroaching famine.

We look inward,
searching for things
that once cheered our souls
and carried us
out of our inertia.

But despite our best efforts
we are now paralyzed,
caught inside a closed circuit
where the grinding wheels
of the future
are fast approaching
the slow turn
of the distant past.

Trapped, we grapple in that loop,
aggrieved in our sorrows,
scratching our old scars,
voicing our usual doubts.

And like a pair of socks
tumbling round and round
in the heat of a dryer,
we've slowly come to feel
that moving in circles
is all there ever will be.

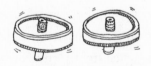

A STRANGE
SMALL SENSE OF ELATION
(NOTE TO SELF)

You were driving north out of New York City on the Taconic State Parkway, toward the Hudson Valley. At one point, the road narrowed rather severely and you encountered a rock wall. It came up on the passenger side without warning. Your hands were clenched tightly on the wheel and your heart raced. *This is a white-knuckle road*, you thought. It didn't take long, though, to get past the rock wall. And when the road widened out again, you felt a sense of relief, a brief hint of what you might even have described as a strange small sense of elation. Odd, because at that point it was the same road you'd been traveling on for more than an hour.

Why weren't you elated then?

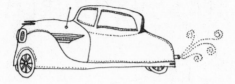

LETTER TO AN UNKNOWN ADDRESS

Dear Susie,

It's been a very long time. So long that I've lost track of where and when it was that I last saw you and when we last spoke. Clearly, you've gone through a lot of changes. There've been many times over the years when I've reached for my phone to call you. But I don't even remember your old number, let alone have your new one! I'm still fluctuating between ecstasy and despair, never quite finding purchase on what people might call the middle ground.

We moved back East two weeks ago. (I know you know that.) It felt like we needed a change. I thought maybe a new environment would be good for me. It was good, at least for the first few weeks. Now I feel rootless. I think I got things wrong. It wasn't that I needed a new physical environment; it was that I needed to do things that are fundamentally new. I'm hopeful, or trying to be hopeful, that opportunities will come.

Can you do me a favor? I imagine you're pretty well positioned to implore God to send blessings to me and Maria and the kids, and to Mom, and to Paul and Nina's families. Can you use your influence? In my opinion, you were an exemplary person, always kind and supportive. You are clearly among the righteous.

God will listen to you. And say hello to Dad from me. I miss you guys.

Love, Peter

ROWS OF SILENCE

My darling L.,

Those dots represent the silences. All those moments between words. All the emotions I feel, which I know you must feel to an even greater degree. You ask if I forgive the woman who accidentally took your mother's life. The truth is that I never blamed her in the first place. Not even for a moment.

I've taken up my anger and my sadness with God. One of the clearest answers I've gotten thus far has been to look at you—so wise and so beautiful—and accept the fact that even though the divine plan isn't the same one I'd have come up with, at least you're here to reflect the bright light that your mother brought to the world.

With love,
Uncle Peter

LEARNING FROM EXPERIENCE

I tried to carry water in a broken bucket
But the water spilled out on the ground
I tried to grow wheat in parched earth
But the wheat withered in the blazing sun
I tried to catch the wind in a burlap sack
But the wind would not be contained
I tried to build trust in a career
But my trust eroded like a sandy shore
I tried to hold faith in a bank account
But my faith waned like a weary moon
I tried to preserve love in self-protection
But my love faded like a dream at dawn

POSSIBLE
(NOTE TO SELF)

How is it possible to pray when you know the
things you've done wrong?
How is it possible to ask for help when you've
wasted so much time?
How is it possible to request a favor when you've
been so ungrateful?
How is it possible to be forgiven
when your thoughts are so impure?
And then you realize that with all your acumen
with all your experience
with all your determination
with all your strength
it remains impossible for you to create even

a single atom
from a single molecule
from a single cell
from the wing of a single gnat.
After all, you are human, and God is God.
And God can always do what for you
is impossible.

THE HOWLING OF COYOTES

It was the fall of 1978 when our family learned that my dad had stage 4 lymphoma. It's difficult to describe the weight of that sort of news. My dad was only forty-eight, a brave former Marine who had become as helpless as a child. I had just turned eighteen, and a life that seemed to be running in a predictable fashion was thrown violently off course. I took to the sadness with gusto, reading every Jerzy Kosiński book I could get my hands on, and to take myself on an even deeper plunge, I pored through *The Drowned and the Saved*, Primo Levi's account of his experiences as a concentration camp victim—not once but twice.

The mood in our house changed, of course. My parents stopped all bickering. There was a seriousness, an electric charge in the air that I'd never felt before. The rush was on to do whatever it took to beat back "the big C," as I'm still wont to call it. Even now, I fear giving strength to the disease by mouthing its name. My plans to move from our family home in Minnesota to New York or Los Angeles to start my music career were forestalled in part by my own fears and in part by a sense of loyalty to the cause of being with my dad, if not helping him to get better.

Early on, there was a doctor's appointment at which it was tersely announced to my dad that he had, at most, six months to live. A man's face whitening at such a verdict is a heavy thing to witness; when that man is your father, it becomes a moment seared into memory. Later, when my dad's salivary glands had been destroyed by radiation, he had to coat his mouth with artificial saliva to eat. It didn't help. Everything he tried tasted like dog food. I ate a small bowl of Purina just to show him that eating could be done, that it must be done.

❑   ❑   ❑

On Thanksgiving night in 1983, our family was gathered at my brother's house. All of us were there save for my dad, who—still alive nearly five years longer than the doctor had initially predicted—was spending Thanksgiving at the hospital. We'd planned on going there later that evening to be with him. During the meal the phone rang. There was something about the sound of that electronic bell—something that signaled the arrival of what we had feared for so long.

The trip to the hospital was filled with a strange and dreamlike beauty. My perceptions were heightened: the sound of my heart pushing hot blood through my body, the elastic wristband of my winter coat pressing on my skin. I was going to a place I had never been. Our father was leaving us that night.

A nurse hesitated in the doorway before coming into the waiting room. "We've done all we can for him," she said.

I was at first immobilized. I sat clinical, distant. The impossible was taking place. Each of my family members was so overcome with anguish that they appeared to me as animals—unrestrained, inhuman in their grief. I watched as their bodies shook in the most terrible way. I listened as they howled and yipped at the top of their lungs. They sounded so much like a pack of coyotes that I could barely repress the urge to laugh. But slowly, once I pushed away my rational mind— that mind that thinks all human hysterics are ridiculous—I stood up from where I was seated and became the loudest coyote of them all.

We buried my dad the next day under a gray November sky. We covered him with shovelfuls of dirt until the casket could no longer be seen and the hole he'd been placed in was level with the ground.

TOM PETTY, 1983

My dad is lying in a bed across town at Mount Sinai Hospital struggling through the final stages of lymphoma, and I'm in our den watching Tom Petty on MTV. Suddenly, and for no apparent reason, my attention is drawn to the round glass light fixture that's been suspended over our dining-room table for the last fifteen years. As I turn to look, the light falls, breaking into thousands of tiny pieces.

That same night I have dream—a nightmare—in which my dad is having a heart attack as I hold him in my arms. He's in pain and he's crying, wetting my chest with his tears. I call out for help. Then I wake up, breathless in the night, my own heart nearly exploding.

In the morning, I visit him in the hospital. He's begun another round of chemotherapy. Almost as soon as I arrive, he grabs for my hand. "Pete," he says. "I'm so afraid!"

I take him in my arms, and he begins to shake. He howls in pain. His tears are wetting my T-shirt, just as they were in my dream, and his thin frame shudders in my grasp. He clutches at his chest, and I can hear myself screaming, "My father is dying! Somebody help! Somebody help me!"

The nurses come running. I stand back, watching as they work. But my mind is elsewhere. I can't stop thinking about that light fixture. Out of nowhere, it just fell. Broken, into thousands of tiny pieces.

NIGHTTIME PRAYER
(NOTE TO SELF)

You lie in bed and think about your day, and you realize that you haven't taken time to slide back a curtain, open a window, or unbolt a door. It was a day without freedom.

You ate, you drank, you fretted, you endured. But you made no attempt to see beyond the confinement you'd trapped yourself in.

You have limited strength, limited talents, limited means, and limited days. The only thing without limits is your ability to love. You can give it all away without its ever diminishing.

And so, in the waning hours of this night, you offer a prayer of thanks for the light that shines on you—for the light that has always shined on you.

SHOVEL

When my brother, Paul, and I were shoveling dirt on our dad's casket, and the only sound was the dull thud of earth on the pine box, I looked over at him and said the most inane thing I could think of. "I love the look of the new Hunt's ketchup bottle." We both laughed. The wonderful thing about juxtaposing opposites is that it makes everything seem so hilarious.

BRAVE FACE

I ask you, does it not come in waves?
"It" being—everything.
And do the days not move like a wheel?
Like a great wheel
Where what is at the top
Soon finds itself at the bottom,
And what is at the bottom
Soon comes to rest at the top?
How should we feel about this—the *all* of it?
Were we not fashioned to abhor these fluctuations?
Does it not take great will and great might
To see beyond our fleeting breaths,
To remain steadfast while those waves roil?
Put on your brave face.
Even in the absence of understanding.
Even amidst abundant fear
And tapering faith.
Put on your brave face.
Even on days of dimming hope
And nights of sorrowful gloaming.
Wear it proudly, beloved sister.
Wear it humbly, my dearest brother,
that it might one day be earned.

LOGGING THE DISTANCE
(NOTE TO SELF)

You know that at every minute of every day, two possible paths present themselves. They are the path of self-gratification and the path of reverence. In considering the length of each, you soon discover that the first never requires more than a journey of, say, half a foot. And the second never requires less than a journey of, say, a million miles. You make your way down each path every day, sometimes logging the distance of your journey to nowhere and sometimes logging the distance of your journey to somewhere.

There's no need to instruct or advise a person on the first path. To traverse its minuscule span is effortless. But the second path requires incredible effort. Along with understanding—and the patience to accept the fact that there can be no understanding at all. How can you understand a thing like the death of a loved one, a burden of such weight? It's impossible to comprehend the pain of it.

Anyone who's walked the second path, even for a short while, knows that it's wise to seek the help of a walking partner, someone to hold hands with and share a story or a laugh with along the way. But you, a person who's been walking the second path for decades, know that it's also imperative to seek the help of a force beyond yourself, a force that can clear the way and whisper words of encouragement as the journey continues.

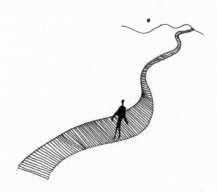

DOWN TO THE BLUFFS

Back in the fall of 1983, during the weeks after my dad died, I had a series of horrible recurring dreams. In them, a team of doctors explains that there is a new treatment for lymphoma available, one with a high likelihood of finally curing my dad. But first they'd have to disinter his body, cut out one or another of his organs, and then start injecting him with a new regimen of drugs. It pains me to say this, but I'd wake up relieved that my dad was dead.

Around that same time, I had a different kind of dream. The dream itself remains one of the happiest experiences of my life. I was riding my bike in the desert, heading toward the ocean. And while I was riding, I heard a voice. Perhaps it was my own.

Drop your disbelief. Allow yourself to be astounded by the sphere of fire overhead. Feel its light and heat on your face as you glide through space. Be aware that you are activating your limbs without any thought or effort. Know that your body is being fueled by nutrients that come from the earth itself. Appreciate that those nutrients seep into your muscles by means of a great mystery called blood. Now look up at the specters of vapor drifting across the sky, those great and beautiful repositories of water. Take in the splendor of it; behold these works of genius!

Today, as I walked down to the bluffs overlooking the Pacific, I realized that I was looking out at the same ocean I'd been riding toward in my dream.

I stood there for a long time, breathing. Just watching the waves and listening to the wind.

OUTSIZE JOY

Not long ago, I lost a favorite scarf of mine. When I found it, in a locker at the Santa Monica YMCA, I held it in my hands for a moment. I was surprised by how happy I was. I wondered then if my outsize joy at finding the scarf was a stand-in for the joy I would feel if were holding Susie or my dad again. Of course, there's no real comparison, but whenever I've found something that I'd assumed was gone forever, even if it was just a scarf, a set of keys, or a wallet, I got a jolt of excitement that was much more powerful than what I was prepared for. Only in a world full of improbability—our world, in fact—could I, a person who daily relies upon facts and science, maintain the belief that I will see my father and my sister again in some form and in some fashion.

This belief, called *T'chiyat Hamaytim* (the revival of the dead), is an idea that is both central to the Jewish faith and widely unfamiliar. Moses Maimonides—physician, philosopher, and renowned Jewish thinker of the Middle Ages—listed belief in the revival of the dead as the final article in his famous Thirteen Articles of Faith. They are as follows:

1. Belief in the existence of the Creator, who is perfect in every way and is the primary cause of all that exists.
2. Belief in God's absolute and unparalleled unity.

3. Belief in God's non-corporeality—the fact that He will not be affected by physical occurrences.
4. Belief in God's eternity.
5. Belief in the imperative to worship God exclusively.
6. Belief in prophecy as God's way of communicating with humans.
7. Belief in the primacy of the prophecy of Moses.
8. Belief in the divine origin of the Torah.
9. Belief in the immutability of the Torah.
10. Belief in God's omniscience and providence.
11. Belief in divine reward and retribution.
12. Belief in the arrival of the Messiah and the messianic era.
13. Belief in the resurrection of the dead.

I don't understand aeronautics, hydraulics, or refrigeration, but still, I have faith that my flight will arrive safely at its destination, my elevator won't fall down the shaft, and my frozen peas will stay frozen. If I were to amplify this idea of *faith without understanding* a thousand times, seeing Susie and my dad once again becomes that much more plausible.

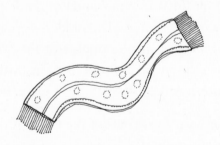

WHITE COATS FOR THE PINES

The night is rimy and raw.
No one is thinking of the trees.
Not of their branches or boughs or
Roots, or their delicate
Needles.

And as a boreal wind tears through the hills,
They stand together,
Saving their strength under
Blue-black skies.

The stars reach out
With their white heat
To warm them,
But as with hope and dreams and God
And other things we
Only sometimes believe in,
The stars were
Too far away to matter much.

And now, when night grows coldest,
When clouds push up
Over the great tips of rock,
Dawn comes slowly, spirit-like,

To cry in empathy and to console
With prayers and tender embraces.

At first light the sky sifts out its finest snow,
Like sugar.
And by early morning
There are white coats for every
Shuddering tree,
To cloak them, yes,
But also to show both of us
How close to the warmth
Of our own blessings we truly are.

HEAVY LEATHER BAG
(NOTE TO SELF)

Y ou've had a leather bag full of fear hanging by a strap over your shoulder for many years. You've been collecting fear in that bag since early childhood, and it's only gotten heavier and more cumbersome. It's no wonder you've got tendinitis. The bag contains several pounds of "I'm not loved unconditionally" and even more of "I always need to appear brilliant so I can be deserving of love" and a whopping supply of "I need to constantly achieve lest I get left behind."

Then there's your suitcase, in which you carry years of insecurity, blame, and childish expectations of the people closest to you. Your palms are blistered from hauling it around.

And on your head you wear an old felt hat, ostensibly to keep the sun off your scalp. But in truth, hidden in a compartment in the crown, you carry a hot little ball of the very worst stuff: anger.

Lately, you've noticed that you've been transporting these things for no good reason. You are not sure what they weigh in total, but you do know that whatever the number is, it's far greater than the pleasure you derive from having them with you. In fact, these things give you no pleasure at all. Perhaps you're curious to know why you haven't realized this before. I guess the answer speaks to one of humankind's most exceptional qualities: the ability to forget.

If you were able to recall your past with clarity, you would remember a time when you weren't dragging that emotional load around—when you weren't a packhorse for your own pain. You started carrying the stuff slowly, little by little, over time. By the age of fifteen or sixteen, you had been carrying the burden so long that you had become inured to its heft. In a very real sense, it had become part of you. Only through some emotional and spiritual amnesia could you believe that letting this burdensome cargo drop from your hands, head, and shoulders would engender horrible consequences. The fact is that you grew to almost cherish the weight. Setting it down would have felt like losing a limb.

You are looking for a blessing, a benediction that will allow you to absorb some lessons about the world and yourself. You know there are just two ways you can receive those blessings: through loss and through joy. When tragedy struck you—and it has—it was as though you'd been looking in a mirror. Only then could you see what you looked like and what you'd been carrying. And when you've experienced great joy—and you have—you stood in front of that same mirror. But in both cases, you caught a glimpse of yourself carrying all those needless and weighty things. Today, you are ready to let them drop to the ground as effortlessly as you would let go of a feather.

And just as easily, you suddenly understand: that is the blessing you've been waiting for.

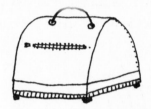

HOW LOST CAN ONE MAN BE?

I've been alive sixty-four years. I'm married to the love of my life. I have four beautiful children, two amazing grandchildren, and the means to accomplish whatever it is I desire. And still, I am sometimes in doubt about the existence of miracles.

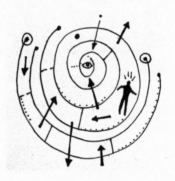

UNTROUBLED DAYS

I am grown. I exist in a frenzy of motion, in a
harried, scattered rush
To get last-minute things done, to set unbalanced
things right,
To get the last song in before the curtain falls,
To fix the dam before the town's aflood,
To fill the hole,
To store the grain,
To stanch the bleeding.
So it's no wonder I sometimes wake up with the
pulse of a runner in the last ten yards.

Master of the Universe, can You see,
Will You see?
I've lost my grip,
Lost my hold on the rope
That ties me to You.

Faith was easy when I was young, when I had only myself to think of, when there were only untroubled days. But now I carry so much and so many days in my mind.

Yes, I am grown, but I am still your child. I am still your child.

AT THE CENTER OF THE WORLD
(NOTE TO SELF)

You sometimes feel groggy and perturbed, and you're never sure why. The morning carries with it not only withering heat but also a portent of something dire. You feel a strange consonance between your burgeoning sense of despair and the exhausting weight of the air itself. You look out over acres of red oak, the leaves of which had only recently unfurled from the entrapment of their buds. Birds of all sorts alight nearby— red-tailed hawks, brightly colored songbirds, cardinals, and madly darting swallows. But despite the beauty, you sit absorbed in a dim melancholy that seems to stem from everywhere and nowhere. You wait there, arrogant and ungrateful, on your terrible perch at the center of the world, unable to wrest yourself away from the dread of an otherwise fine day.

Many hours later, just as the afternoon is turning toward dusk, dark clouds begin hurtling across the sky from the west—colossal things, imperious, hurrying to darken the day. Then from the north, the lightning comes. Fiery bolts hurl downward from the top of the heavens to the tops of the distant hills. And in the aftermath of each strike comes ground-shaking thunder, rumbling with a depth that causes your heart to race. Next, a torrential rain falls, and the arid ground is turned instantly to mud. And as the dark clouds release their oceans of rain, as the lightning bisects the dome of the sky, and as the thunder persists in roiling the ground beneath you, you realize with suddenness, and with great relief, that you are free, that you were never at the center of anything at all.

SPLIT SCREEN

NOVEMBER 21, 2010
PITTSBURGH, PENNSYLVANIA

It's late Sunday afternoon. A cold wind rises off the Allegheny River and snakes around the tall buildings that ring the heart of the city. It blows so hard that the white prayer shawl that serves as a wedding canopy is in danger of blowing into the dimming sky. My friend Ezra's son stomps on the glass, the guests shout "Mazal tov," and soon everyone is clapping and singing.

I can't keep from smiling as Ezra beams. And just before his son leaves the stage with his new bride, I watch as he kisses Ezra gently on the forehead. Ezra's brother and son-in-law each take one of his arms. If they were to let go for even a moment, he would fly off into the heavens from sheer joy.

As his son and his new bride melt into the crowd, Ezra takes his wife's hand and sings, almost in a whisper—or as an afterthought. The sound that passes from his lips is unearthly.

I look down at my watch; it's exactly quarter to five.

NOVEMBER 28, 2010
CITY OF COMMERCE, CALIFORNIA

It's late Sunday afternoon. A cold wind rises off the San Bernardino Mountains and snakes around the low-slung warehouses that ring the cemetery. It blows so hard that the white tarp protecting the newly dug dirt from an imminent rain is in danger of blowing into the dimming sky. There's nothing green here—no trees, no comfort or consolation. This is, after all, the place where my friend Noah will bury his dead son.

I can't keep from crying as Noah covers his face, and just before the first of the mourners climbs the small pile of dirt to take hold of the shovels, I watch as he stumbles. Noah's brother and son-in-law each take one of his arms. If they were to let go even for a moment, he would fall into the open grave.

As the first scoop of dirt hits his son's casket, Noah drops to his knees and moans, almost in a whisper—or as an afterthought. The sound that passes from his lips is unearthly.

I look down at my watch, and strangely, now, too, it's exactly quarter to five.

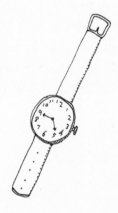

PRAYER FOR A MORNING WITH MANY SHADOWS
(NOTE TO SELF)

Tether me to my purpose today. Don't let me go adrift. Strengthen me to push beyond my insistence on my own limitations.

Help me find a door in the circle I've drawn around myself. Help me escape the iron cage that causes a soul to wither in isolation.

All that poses as reality—let it have no dominion over me. The myriad idols that parade before me—let them have no sway.

You are in hiding, yet I search for You. You both transcend and inhabit your own creation. Opaque layers conceal your mystery. Help me peel them back—but not all the way, of course.

Just enough so that I can feel your presence.

SUNSET

This morning we were young.

But by late afternoon, as the sun became shrouded in afternoon fog, we had aged.

And soon afterward, when that same sun lowered itself into the Pacific, even our thoughts felt old.

"One day we will see how this all works," I said.

"For now, though, we needn't think about it much," you replied.

As if either of us could make sense of it.

How youthful color turns a pallid gray, how backs rippling with vigor become weak, how energy sneaks away—elsewhere.

While we can, we must run.

We must run into our long night laughing and singing.

And at this moment, we must grasp for both laughter and song.

PART III

TEACHERS

Chord suggestion: A major

When you're writing a song, it's helpful to connect with thoughts of people who have inspired you. They are your best defense against the voices of self-judgment, voices that whisper that what you have to say is not worthy of being heard.

WOMAN WITH THE STRENGTH OF TEN THOUSAND MEN

I was fortunate to have several mentors in my life, people who could sense the seeds of what I could become and nurture them during my times of doubt. My uncle Sonny is foremost among these mentors of mine.

Sonny, a.k.a. Arthur Turovh Himmelman, is my dad's younger brother. My dad was sixteen years old on the day Sonny was born. Because Sonny was the indisputable baby of the family, the name stuck. Sonny did many things that made him exceptional in my eyes as I was growing up—and make him exceptional today. He was a member of Mensa; he smoked pot with me when I was fourteen; he gave me a copy of John Lee Hooker's double album *Endless Boogie*; he turned me on to Bob Dylan; he talked frankly with me about sex; he talked with me about God—and without any pressure at all, shared his opinion that there is no such thing. But more than all that, my uncle Sonny listened to me. And by listening, I don't mean the perfunctory kind of listening that teenagers expect from adults. He was there with me whenever we spoke.

When I was in ninth grade and nearly failing out of junior high, Sonny played the role of diplomat and ambassador between my parents and me. When they were at their wit's end, not knowing what to do to help me become a normal kid, Sonny came to them with a bold idea. "Why not rent Peter an apartment in Uptown?" he asked, referring to a formerly seedy area just southwest of downtown Minneapolis. "You can let him use it as a kind of artist's retreat, a getaway where he can pursue his creative ambitions." I wasn't in the room while this conversation was taking place, but knowing that the end result was a resounding "No," I can only imagine the looks on my parents' faces when Sonny proffered the suggestion.

Sonny was alleged to have put forward this simple truth to my parents as well: "You've gotta understand—Peter's not your typical suburban Jewish kid. He's not going to be a doctor, a lawyer, or an accountant. He's going to be a musician." As I said, this conversation did not result in my parents' renting me an apartment in Uptown, or anywhere else for that matter, but the fact that there was someone who understood my feelings even before I did—and certainly before I could articulate them—made my life much better.

When a young person dreams of the future, the likelihood that those dreams will fade away with time is great. But what Sonny did for me, and what makes him such a beloved and valued person in my life, is that he fought alongside me to ensure that those dreams didn't fade. Because of his insights and encouragement, they not only didn't fade but also became stronger over the years. When I'd play shows at local clubs and coffeehouses in and around the Twin Cities, Sonny would make a point to be in the audience at every gig. After each one, he'd come backstage to tell me what he liked about the performance, what moved him most. That technique is, incidentally, the best way to give feedback to fledgling artists. By telling them what you like about their work—assuming you like anything—you also tell them, painlessly, what you don't like.

◻ ◻ ◻

By the spring of 1989, I'd released three albums for Island Records, none of which sold particularly well, although they'd each garnered enough positive critical attention to make the label interested in keeping me around for a fourth. The trouble was that the label's president, Lou Maglia, the gruff, old-school record guy who'd signed me, had just left the label. I was at a crossroads. If I stuck around, it was likely that the incoming president, Mike Bone, might see me as just detritus from the old regime and give zero attention to my new record. On the other hand, if I asked to leave the label, it was equally likely that I'd have tremendous difficulty getting a new label to pick me up.

I've never been sure whether it's confidence, desperation, or just an impulse to roll the dice that fuels my willingness to take chances, but a few weeks after Mike Bone took the helm of Island Records, I gathered up all the accounting statements I'd received from the label and went to see him. I spread the statements out on Mike's desk and said, "You can see I'm deep in the red. I'd like you to release me."

"You sure about that?" Mike asked.

I walked out of his office labelless but also a free agent.

I had been recently married and was flying nonstop between Los Angeles, New York, and Minneapolis that winter, trying to figure out my next move, when I got a call from Sonny. He told me there was someone he wanted me to meet.

"Who is it?" I asked.

"You'll see when we get there" was all the information he offered.

I flew to Minneapolis to finish some demos I'd been recording, and Sonny picked me up at my brother's house, in Minnetonka. We drove together across the Mississippi River to Saint Paul, parked outside a small house, and walked quietly into a darkened, mostly unfurnished living room, save for some folding chairs and a hospital gurney that was set up in the middle of the room. In the gurney, propped up on several large pillows and facing two large computer screens, was a dark-haired, extremely thin woman around my uncle's age. Whoever she was, she was clearly facing a serious health issue. She couldn't move or speak, and I was uncomfortable not knowing exactly how, or if, I should address her, so I just watched.

The woman's name, I soon learned, was Susan Margoles. Susan was in the advanced stages of ALS. She had been a beautiful woman before her illness, and it was easy to see traces of that beauty, even in her devastated condition. I also learned that she had once danced professionally and that she was known, and sometimes feared, for her acerbic wit.

In addition to a feeding tube, which ran under the white bedsheets and blankets on her gurney, there was an electrical cord of some kind patched into the computer monitor on one end, with the other end of the cord taped to Susan's left eyebrow. On the screen were letters from the alphabet, constantly whizzing by.

A-B-C-D-E-F-G-H-I-J-K-L-M-N-O…

Susan was able to carefully—painfully, it seemed—spell out words by selecting letters with her eyebrow, which was the only muscle still unaffected by the disease. This was her sole means of communication. It was her lifeline to the outside world. She lay on her bed, answering questions from my uncle and the others who were present. For the most part, I kept quiet and stared in fascination as she carried on a thoughtful, albeit extremely slow, conversation.

There was a fish tank in the living room, off in the corner, containing fish I didn't recognize. I finally mustered the courage to ask her about them. She began typing her answer to me, letter by letter.

T H E S E A R E B R A C K I S H W A T E R F I S H

Despite the severe challenges she was confronted with, I felt that Susan was doing her best to make *me* feel comfortable. I spoke with her a bit about my own experience raising Mozambique mouthbrooders as a teenager. I said that eventually I had to flush them down the toilet because of strict state laws about introducing nonindigenous fish into Minnesota waterways—not to mention the fact that no aquarium shop wanted to take them because of the tremendous size they were known to grow to.

I K N O W T H A T F I S H, she wrote. V E R Y B I G

I was beginning to understand that I was in the presence of someone very special, someone with a worldview that, partly because of her tragic circumstances, was profoundly different from my own and likely from most everyone else's on the planet. This had to have been why Sonny was so adamant that I meet her and why he kept referring to Susan as an "Olympian of the spirit."

Out of nowhere, one of the people sitting next to me, a sort of religious zealot, it seemed, started in on an annoying quasi-spiritual rant. I knew immediately where it was going, and I shuddered when he got to his insane and cruel punch line. In the strident tone that only an oblivious zealot can muster, he coughed up this chestnut: "You know, Susan, God doesn't give you more than you can handle."

Susan had already begun typing away at her response. We were all silent, waiting for whatever it was that she could possibly have to say. It wasn't long before we'd all gotten a dose of her wonderfully caustic humor. She typed out two words.

O Y V E Y

If you're not Jewish, or haven't heard the expression "Oy vey," you should know that it's not an easy one to interpret. But I'll give it a go. "Oy vey" is used to indicate incredulity about something one has heard or experienced. It is a groan and a sigh. It is a lament about the state of the world. It is, perhaps most of all, a succinct way to express profound displeasure about something beyond one's control. We all sat there looking at what Susan had written up on the screen. There was some nervous laughter—because after all, despite her horrible situation, it was funny. And "Oy vey" was also her brilliant, super-Jewish way of saying, "I'm tired; let's wrap this up." The zealot was escorted out of the house first, and the rest of us soon followed.

❏ ❏ ❏

The creative process is very much like the process of human reproduction. There is a moment of conception, which in the creative process is what I experienced the moment I saw Susan write her short, powerful message. For me, witnessing a woman with ALS type a humorous and discreet message—one that carried with it both her humanity and the mystery embodied in the classic question "Why do the righteous suffer?"—was very much akin to the implantation of sperm inside an ovum. It was a fertilization. To call it a seminal moment is as precise a definition as possible.

The insight I had in the room with Susan grew within me until, like a fetus, it reached its due date. But instead of a child, what came out was a song called "Woman with the Strength of Ten Thousand Men."

Shortly after I received my release from Island Records, I made the rounds of several other record labels in New York and received only a smattering of interest. The label that was most interested in me happened to be the one that I was most interested in, too—Epic Records, which had just been sold to Sony. As an artist with only a middling sales record, I was surprised when an A&R man named Michael Caplan took a very brave chance on me in the summer of 1990. I socked away the advance money I'd gotten from Epic, and instead of renting time in a professional recording studio, as was almost always done at the time, I bought an entire studio's worth of recording equipment, equipment that would soon comprise my own studio. This was extremely unorthodox for a new artist, and Michael Caplan was assailed with questions from Epic's legal affairs people as to whether this was permissible. Apparently it was, because I was soon recording on the new gear. The music was sounding good, and no further discussion of the topic ensued.

Among the songs that became must-haves for my Epic debut, *From Strength to Strength*, was "Woman with the Strength of Ten Thousand Men." I'd recorded the track, mixed it, and mastered it. The album-cover artwork had been approved. And then, in the middle of the night, I awoke with a start. I never approved the song with Susan Margoles! The next morning, I made a few calls to Minnesota to track her down. My uncle Sonny helped as well. We found out that Susan's condition had worsened and that she had been transferred to a hospital.

Within a day or two, I was speaking with Susan's attending nurse. I explained who I was and why I was calling. I asked the nurse if I could speak with Susan, and she put the phone up to Susan's ear. "This is Peter Himmelman," I said. "You might not remember me, but I was the guy who came to visit you with Arthur Himmelman. I asked you about your brackish-water fish." There was no response, of course, and so I continued. "I'm a songwriter, and I wrote a song about you that's going to come out on an album this fall. I just wanted to know if I have your permission to release it."

The nurse got on the line and told me that Susan was typing. After several minutes, she said, "Susan says she wants you to come to Minnesota and play her the song."

A trip to Saint Paul would be extremely inconvenient for me. I had an infant son and a spate of touring on my schedule that wouldn't take me anywhere near Minnesota. But far worse than the inconvenience was the frightening prospect of playing my song live for Susan in her hospital room. It began to dawn on me just how presumptuous and insensitive it was of me to have assumed that Susan would allow me to make this very personal song about her available to the public. I soon headed for LAX, guitar case in hand.

Uncle Sonny was already there when I arrived at the hospital, and we walked slowly together down the hallway to Susan's room, trying to prepare for, as Sonny joked, the toughest audition of my life. We knocked softly, and the nurse I'd spoken with on the phone led us inside. Susan's face was gaunt, her skin sallow. I managed a timid hello, then unpacked my guitar. Since I hadn't memorized the lyrics, I spread them out on the foot of Susan's bed and began a halting, subdued rendition of the song.

After a long, uncomfortable silence, Susan began typing out her verdict. I knew then that I had overstepped my bounds. I had been egotistical, impetuous, and thoughtless in assuming that putting the song on my new record was a good idea—never mind the presumption it took to write the song itself. Although the first word Susan began to type out on her computer was incomplete, its meaning was plain for all to see.

B E A, she'd written.

I hadn't forgotten her swift, razorlike dismemberment of the zealot several months previously. Now it was my turn. B E A T I T is what I expected to read. But Susan started typing again, and we waited—the nurse, Sonny, and I. When she finished her sentence, I read the most gratifying words that have ever been written about my work.

B E A U T F U L I N S I G H T I N T O H O W I F E E L

▢ ▢ ▢

Susan died not long after that day. The record was released that fall as planned. "Woman with the Strength of Ten Thousand Men" was its first single. The recording of the song was played at Susan's funeral.

I received the following letter from Susan's brother, Alan, on January 10, 2019, nearly thirty years after I'd written the song. (The letter was written in response to an account of my meeting with Susan that I'd published online that same year.) With his permission, I have reproduced it here.

Peter, I am Alan Margoles, the brother of Susan Margoles.

I was so grateful to read your wonderful story. Everything you related about your meetings with her, including her insistence that you fly to Minneapolis to personally perform your wonderful song for her, was classic Suzy. ALS took away virtually all her physical abilities, but it sharpened her only remaining instrument, her intellect.

As the disease progressed, Suzy became much more focused on her individual rights as well as the rights and independence of others with similar disabilities.

At the time Suzy was incapacitated there was limited access to home health care, and she decided to do something about it. Although she could control only her eyes and one eyebrow, she managed to establish and codirect a nonprofit organization that helps people with disabilities qualify for funding for health-care services in their own homes, giving them the independence and quality of life that cannot be provided in a hospital setting. Her strength, determination, and, yes, her bossiness led her to testify in Washington, DC, before the House of Representatives, using only her eyebrow switch and letter board to communicate. She made them listen.

That same notorious in-your-face persistence encouraged scores of other people with disabilities to contact her for assistance. With her knowledge of funding alternatives and home-care options, she was able to get many individuals out of nursing homes and hospital situations and into home health-care settings, where they could be themselves…have a pet, entertain loud visitors or children at any hour, and otherwise regain parts of life they had lost in an institutional setting.

You probably already know much of the information I just related. But what you may not know is how much you and your song meant to Suzy. She never cared about accolades, but your visits with her were very personal and meaningful. We still have Little Fleetwood, the boom box that you generously brought to her apartment and left with her, complete with the cassette tape of "Woman with the Strength of Ten Thousand Men" inside.

Dignity and the ability to be understood are precious commodities to people with severe disabilities. Suzy paid you her highest compliment when she credited you with insight into how she felt. My family thanks you for singing about the Suzy we knew rather than the disability she battled for so long.

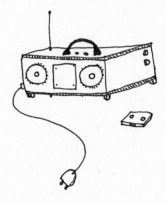

BLUES SINGER

In 1986, as now, the most effective way to promote a new musical act was to have it open for an established artist. Lou Maglia, the newly installed president of Island Records at the time, and the guy who signed me to the label in the early stages of my career, had been considering a few possibilities for me: Sting, for example, as well as Joe Cocker and some others. But one day, I walked into Lou's office and closed the door behind me. I was about to forgo each of those opportunities in a single fifteen-minute meeting.

I didn't balk or sugarcoat what I had to say. There was no need to. I was at a place in my life when not following my gut would have been like punching my mom in the nose. In that sense, it wasn't a choice.

"Lou," I said, "I'm starting to keep this Jewish thing called Shabbos, and I won't be available to perform on Friday nights any longer."

Lou looked at me for a moment, then just belly laughed. Not to be cruel or condescending—he wasn't that kind of guy. Lou simply had no language, no context, for what he'd just heard. It's likely he couldn't grasp even a bit of what I was saying. He only laughed because he'd assumed I was joking. And it *was* funny. Why would an artist who'd worked so hard to get to this point in his career tell the president of a major record label that he wouldn't work on a Friday night—the most important show-business night of the week?

I wish I could tell you that my spiritual awakening, if you want to call it that, was about being caught up in a moment of tremendous joy, but it wasn't. It was a somber, serious thing. In some ways it was linked with thoughts of mortality. Strange as it may sound, there is a deep sense of fulfillment in the realization that death is pervasive and imminent, even as we pretend it's not there. That is, it's only possible to feel acutely the gratification of one's own aliveness when life and death are set side by side, when they are in contrast with each other.

❑ ❑ ❑

In the winter of 1984, a little more than a year before my meeting with Lou, I was sitting in a cramped apartment in South Minneapolis auditioning some songs I'd written for a local rhythm-and-blues singer named Doug Maynard. As I went through a dozen or so songs, Doug nursed a beer, listening and nodding quietly—he was a hell of a singer, but not much of a talker.

Suddenly he perked up. At last, something I played caught his attention. "Man, I think I could do this one justice," he said. It was a simple funk-tinged thing called "My First Mistake": *You taste like pepper frosting on a granite cake / Baby, fallin' in love with you was my first mistake…* I was twenty-four. It was a huge day for me, knowing that a local musical hero dug one of my songs and was going to perform it in his set. Things were moving, changing.

Less than a year later, Doug was found dead in his living room at the age of forty. But before this happened, he was gracious enough to have introduced me to his manager, who introduced me to a New York City music lawyer, who introduced me to a record producer named Kenny Vance. Kenny was cool. Still is. He'd worked with a lot of people, famous people, and he wasn't particularly shy about mentioning who they were.

One evening, after everyone had cleared out of the studio where we'd been recording some demos, Kenny and I sat for an hour or so, ate some macrobiotic food from a place he knew down the street, and shared a little bit about ourselves. "I used to date Diane Keaton," he told me. "I know Woody Allen—been in a couple of his films. I know Donald Fagen of Steely Dan. I was the music director for *Saturday Night Live*. I know Lenny Waronker, the former head of Warner Brothers Records. But tonight," he said, "I'm gonna take you to my main connection, a religious Jew in Brooklyn."

Later that night, Kenny and I traveled to an apartment in Crown Heights, where his friend Rabbi Simon Jacobson greeted us. I liked Simon right off the bat. His eyes reflected some essential paradox, some awareness that being alive is both a source of great humor and great sadness. His brilliant wife, Shaindy, a petite and attractive woman around my age, introduced herself with a gracious smile and placed glass bowls of almonds and chocolate-covered coffee beans on a yacht-size table before excusing herself to tend to their young children.

The thing I didn't understand at first was how a big, hirsute guy like Simon, with his oversize yarmulke, massive beard, and buttoned-up white polyester shirt, was able to land such a good-looking woman. But I soon learned that in Crown Heights, it isn't the guy who can throw a football the farthest who gets the girl. Simon had another thing going for him. He's what you could rightly call a genius.

Simon's job at the time was to memorize every word of the Lubavitcher Rebbe's talks during Shabbat—a time when the use of electronic recording devices is forbidden—and, with the help of his small staff, write them down from memory on Saturday night for publication later in the week. When the Lubavitcher Rebbe spoke, it was often for four or more hours straight—without breaks, without notes, and in a cyclical manner of increasing complexity.

It grew late, and just past 1:00 a.m., a tired Kenny said his goodbyes and drove back to Manhattan. I stayed on as Simon continued speaking. I kept looking up at the simple oil paintings of the Rebbe hanging on the walls. I was prodded more by fatigue than bravado when I finally asked, "What's the deal with those pictures of the Rebbe? They seem sort of cultish to me."

Simon was not at all defensive. "I enjoy the pictures," he said. "To me, the Rebbe is like a very inspiring grandfather, and I get a lot out of reflecting on the things he says and the way he lives his life." This made some sense to me.

Then Simon paused, looking across the table at me. When he saw I was focused on him, he continued. "There are people for whom there is no sense of self," he said. "People called *tzadikim*, and they have no need for personal gain. *Tzadikim* live only to serve others, and they can do anything they wish."

"Really?" I asked with a hint of comic disdain. "Can they fly?"

"Understand," Simon said without irony, "that I've never seen anyone fly. But for a *tzadik*, the act of flying is no greater miracle than the act of walking."

This idea stunned me. Not because it was new or complicated. The things that truly move us rarely are. No, I was stunned because when you stop to think about it, there's absolutely no difference between the two miracles, walking and flying. It's just that we non-*tzadikim* get tired of the one because we do it all the time.

For some strange reason, at that moment, sitting at that table in Brooklyn, I started thinking about the little-known rhythm-and-blues singer Doug Maynard. I was remembering the sound of his voice and considering the infinite number, the impossible number, of tiny choices and coincidences—the gossamer filaments, if you will—that wove together to guide me to that apartment on that particular night. The thought was so vivid that it was as if I could hear Doug singing again. Singing most soulfully, most truthfully, about the joy, the fear, and the pain of this world.

EFFORTLESSLY
(NOTE TO SELF)

You are always in motion, constantly battling forces you can't describe, constantly pulling or pushing on a weight that won't budge. Sometimes, as you brush your teeth at night, you look in the mirror and catch a glimpse of yourself. There's something about seeing yourself stare at your own face that makes you turn away. It's frightful to see yourself like that, especially at the end of a long and tiring day, when resistance is nearly nonexistent and when defenses against things strange and troubling are at their nadir.

And so you turn away from the mirror, only to look quickly back. The first thing you see is how much older you've become. And though you are still, in some ways, handsome, you see only the ways in which you've aged. For you, this is more than a simple aesthetic appraisal. You are coming to terms with the fact that the face looking back at you, the eyes that you've seen countless times, the eyes that have allowed you to see countless things, will one day no longer be. And as you dress for bed and lie back on your pillow, you look up at the smoke alarm on the ceiling, as you often do, and watch the tiny red light for a while, as if it were a miniature planet hanging millions of miles above you.

The moon, visible now outside your window, is not quite full but still surreally bright on this cloudless night. You feel a great pang of loss and mystery. The wind rushes in from the north, warm and scented with freshly cut hay. You can tell from the air that a heavy rain is soon on its way. You stretch your legs in bed and feel the covers light upon your skin.

You notice the strange sensation of the past being both distant and near. You remember, as a child, feeling comforted by the sound of your mother and father speaking to each other in the living room, just down the hall from your room, their voices rising sometimes and at other times falling, like music. Back then, it was easy to believe in God. God was like your parents, only much bigger, much wiser. But as you grew up, you came, through a series of misfortunes, to believe that neither God nor your parents could provide you with the safety and love you knew you required and deserved.

"This is what growing old is," you used to say. "It's just trading false assumptions for other false assumptions." But tonight, as you look slowly back and forth from the tiny red-light planet to the moon, you realize that growing old isn't about embracing new lies or surrendering to bitter truths. It's about letting go of disbelief, which is, you now think, the greatest and gravest false assumption of all.

And as you close your eyes, you mouth a silent prayer that comes to you—like everything you've ever truly believed in—effortlessly. It goes like this:

> *God, I grew to conceive of You as a child's fantasy. Now I see that the fantasy was to assume that it was You who was not real and that the world around me, the world I can taste and touch, was real. Please forgive me—and I feel that You do. I feel that your love for me and for the world, which You bring to life at every moment, is reality. The only plausible reality. Please let me rest on this night that is both regular and deeply hallowed. Please allow my soul to ascend as I sleep, and like a painter who refreshes her brush, please dip my spirit in bright colors once again so I might paint a new life for myself on the canvas of tomorrow, your sacred gift to the living. Let me hear your voice echo down the hallway as my parents' voices once did, when I was young and full of innocence, full of acceptance, full of grace. Full of peace.*

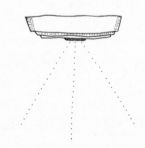

FREEDOM IN RESTRICTION

I felt a kind of heat rising around me in the years after my dad died, a sense that what had long been static was stuttering back into motion. There was a pleasant strangeness to the feeling, but like many things that at first seem unusual, it wasn't wholly unfamiliar. I'd felt that same sensation when I was lying awake in my bed in the dark as a young child, focusing on individual moonlit snowflakes as they fell outside my window. I felt it again in Jerusalem, at the age of nine, when I first touched the sunbaked stones of the Wailing Wall. I felt it the first time I snorkeled in the Red Sea and became drunk from its sheer beauty. I felt it the frigid November morning we buried my father.

The circumstances were wildly varying, but in each instance there was a sense of being taken from one place to another, of inertia finally giving way to movement. It was as if my life had cracked open and I saw arrayed in front of me something of the unseen hand that forms and directs the universe.

When I was twenty-six, I came to know, with a certainty I hadn't felt before, perhaps couldn't have felt, that I needed to get married. I had awakened to the idea that there was nothing in my life—not music, not friendships, not that almighty record deal—more important than finding the right woman to start a family with and live out my days with. I also knew that to do this, I needed to create a powerful framework for myself, one that would allow me to channel my outsize ego and creative energies into building a stable future.

So I made a pact with myself, an unwritten personal agreement. It came down to this simple declaration: *The next time I sleep with a woman, it will be with my future wife.* In short, I had to make a fundamental behavioral and emotional shift. I would need to wean myself away from years of assumptions about the nature of what a modern male-female relationship is. I would have to forge a new way of looking at women, at my role as a man, and at the world at large.

It became clear to me that the freedom I had always longed for could be obtained only through the somewhat paradoxical means of setting limits, delaying gratification, and avoiding many experiences that an all-pervasive consumer culture was (and is) hell-bent on selling.

Allow me to explain this further by way of a musical analogy.

I would argue that music is among the most transcendent of all art forms, both for the performer and for the listener. Since it has no form or substance, I would also argue that it's the most spiritual. But as anyone who has mastered a musical instrument knows, musical expressions are created almost exclusively by means of structure and constriction, things that very few of us would correlate with freedom.

At first glance, this seems like a paradox. How could something as liberating as music be based on constriction? Well, not only is music *based* on constriction, I'd also go so far as to say that, aside from the existence of raw sound—elemental white noise, if you will—the only thing that allows music to be born, the only thing that differentiates it from random noise, is the musician's choice of what gets left behind. In this sense, music comes about not by choosing notes but by eliminating them. Only by rejecting all other sonic choices are we left with the ones we truly desire. To make music, we don't add: we subtract. When an accomplished pianist plays the piano, she is, in effect, leaving behind the notes she wishes to eliminate.

Most, if not all, musical instruments work on this principle of elimination. The sound of a trumpet, for example, requires compression and constriction. If the air a player blows into the mouthpiece weren't compressed and regulated by the embouchure, then all you would hear is a soft, wind-like noise passing through the metal.

As I became increasingly immersed in spiritual thought and practice, the idea of freedom in restriction became clearer and more personally meaningful to me. If this idea were true for music, I wondered, how much more so must it be for all of life itself? And given that human sexuality (whether the participants engaging in an intimate act are conscious of it or not) concerns the creation of life, it occurred to me that causing dissonance in this most essential—dare I say mystical?—realm was something I definitely needed to avoid.

I knew I had to place a set of limitations on myself in order to make music out of my life. I became alert to a perception I recalled vaguely from early childhood. It was as if I could see something important forming out of a fleeting sliver of thought, as it did when I was lying, feverish, in bed, waiting for sleep.

It was frightening as an adult to feel these thoughts, but it also felt safe in some ways, as though there'd been a revelation that seemed to say:

> *Peter, son of David, there is a purpose to everything you've experienced in the recent past and everything you see before you now. Twenty-six years ago, you came down to inhabit another plane. You descended from the place where your father is now, a world of souls, where everything is as intangible as thought and as abstract and formless as light. And now, from this moment on, there are things you must do and ways you must act.*

The mantra "live without limitations," which had guided me for most of my life, was at that point leading me only to chaos. I believed I could and must do better for myself. My most fervent wish was no longer to become a rock star; it was to create a family, one that could become a replacement for the one I'd been missing, the one that had changed so drastically when my father died. So, on a tour bus rolling across the North American continent, I did the three most practical things I could think of: I stuck to my private pact, I dreamed, and I prayed several times a day for strength and for love.

WHAT GOD IS NOT

God isn't a spirit any more than God is a carrot, a chunk of ice, or an airplane propeller. Nor is God an ephemeral energy, a celestial being, or a He or a She. Everything we can imagine, no matter how small or how lofty, is merely a created entity. God alone was *not* created; God is a first cause.

Think of it this way: God is the only creator, and everything else—including seraphs, skim milk, and the Dewey Decimal System—are all creations. Human beings make lots of things, but we don't really create in the purest sense; we amalgamate. Even the most brilliant artists and inventors appropriate previously created things and change their forms. But there's something fundamentally different about the way God creates. When God creates, it's called in Latin *creatio ex nihilo*, or, in the English translation, *creation from nothing at all*.

Carl Sagan, the world-famous astronomer, once asked this question: "What's the first step you'd take if you were making an apple pie?" Most of us would probably say, "Peel some apples." But Sagan wasn't satisfied with that answer. His answer was: "First, create the heavens and the earth."

ROCKS DON'T FLY

A man looks out his window and sees a rock in midflight. "The rock is flying," he says. The wise man next to him says, "The rock is not flying. It only appears to be in flight. When the force exerted upon the rock by the one who threw it ceases to have any effect, the rock will fall to the ground and return to its true condition of flightlessness."

Similarly, the universe as we know it is not flying. It is not existing. It only *appears* to exist. God is the hidden rock thrower. The world is not fundamentally real, nor are the things most of us consider real. Like the flying rock, they are utterly dependent upon God for their existence. If the force of God's willing the universe into existence were to stop, everything we know would disappear, just as our dreams do when we awaken.

God is praying, willing, and dreaming the universe into being at every moment.

KNOWING
(NOTE TO SELF)

You've been acculturated to have answers. But is it possible that not having answers is in some ways better?

At this moment, you are thinking of what you're doing (which happens to be writing), but if you pay close attention, you'll be able to sense many more layers of thought, most of which will remain unknown, even as they engender strong feelings. These mysterious layers of thought may surface later as dreams. They might also surface in times of great emotion—perhaps not as words, but again, as feelings without names. In this sense, you hardly know yourself at all. And if this is so, should you not conclude that you know even less about the world?

It's not that you don't know things. Of course you do. You've memorized and categorized thousands of ideas.

Right off the top of your head, here are ten that you're certain of:

1. Trees bear fruit, but not always.

2. The sun provides warmth.

3. Birds fly, generally speaking.

4. Spanish is a language spoken mostly in Spain as well as in several countries in Latin America and South America.

5. It is good to be free from war and disease.

6. Love feels better than loneliness.

7. Peaches have a layer of fuzz on the outside.

8. Most fish can breathe underwater.

9. There are three primary colors: red, blue, and yellow.

10. People sometimes cry when their emotions are beyond the power of words.

But do you really know these things? Or does your so-called knowledge merely skim the surface of what there is to know about them?

1. Trees bear fruit, but not always.

   Yes, but how does a sapling become a tree and not an egg? And why do some trees bear fruit and others don't?

2. The sun provides warmth.

   Yes, but what exactly is warmth, particularly in the absence of a living thing to sense it?

3. Birds fly, generally speaking.

   Yes, but aside from casually using the word "flight," as if you know what it means, what do you actually know about the experience of flight? And furthermore, how does the act of flight define the creature we refer to as a bird?

4. Spanish is a language spoken mostly in Spain as well as in several countries in Latin America and South America.

   Yes, but what, if anything, characterizes a language as specifically "Spanish"?

5. It is good to be free from war and disease.

   Except for the assumption that most human beings dislike war and disease, what makes freedom from war and disease objectively "good"?

6. Love feels better than loneliness.

   Yes, love may feel better than loneliness for most human beings, but what about love makes it feel better than loneliness? And since we can only define love and lone-

liness in terms of the way humans, and perhaps certain animals, feel, are we really able to define either thing?

7. Peaches have a layer of fuzz on the outside.

   Yes, but "fuzz" is a term that's relative to the size of the organism sensing it. For example, is it possible that the fairyfly, which is nearly four hundred times smaller than a typical ant and around two or three times the width of a human hair, might sense the fuzz as something more like a field of spikes?

8. Most fish can breathe underwater.

   Yes, but what is the essence of breath, whether above the water or beneath its surface?

9. There are three primary colors: red, blue, and yellow.

   Yes, but are colors a reality? Or are they simply sensations in the minds of humans and animals?

10. People sometimes cry when their emotions are beyond the power of words.

    Yes, but what, exactly, is the power of words? And why do tears come out of our eyes when we experience deep emotions?

The more you think about this, the more it becomes clear that you haven't learned anything new about the things you purport to know—other than how to categorize and organize them within your own limited mental framework. And as you gradually realize—and grudgingly admit—that most of your "knowledge" is not only incomplete but also minuscule, it occurs to you that the things you "know" are often the very things that stop you from obtaining a deeper knowledge and awareness of yourself and the world.

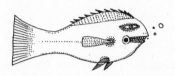

THE MAN IN THE DIRTY SHROUD

It was early morning when I arrived in New York City. The temperature was already racing upward. By 2:00 p.m., it was more than one hundred degrees in the shade. After dropping off some packages at the FedEx facility, I spotted an old man sleeping in the middle of the sidewalk in the blazing heat, wearing what looked like a dirty shroud. He'd piled his possessions into paper grocery bags on either side of him. Dozens of pedestrians walked past as he lay there: some looked straight ahead, some chatted noisily on their phones, some did both.

At that moment, three disturbing questions seized me: *How long will it take me to become inured to this small but very real tragedy playing out on 111th Street and Broadway? How many destitute people will I have to see before I, too, walk by with total disregard for their tragic situation? What mental and spiritual processes will seduce me into becoming just another passerby, deadened to the pain of a fellow human being?* I'd like to claim that as a moment of enlightenment. But I knew that very soon I'd resemble everyone else dashing past the tragedy of this shroud-clad man, glued to my phone and absorbed in all the "important" things I needed to accomplish. I might as well have put on a shroud of my own.

Already I felt myself succumbing to numbness, the forces of unconcern masquerading as deep concern for daily errands. When I saw the shroud-clad man lying there, my empathy hadn't fully deserted me, not yet. But I did come face-to-face with empathy's fragility. I left five dollars beside him. I knew it wouldn't help much, and I didn't do it for his benefit anyway—just for my own. It was like watching a bulb dim and the world tilt toward darkness—my humanity receding, becoming less vital.

I justify my actions as I tune out the pain of strangers in need. I declare the tuning out a necessary evil because I gain something with my loss of empathy: the ability to move briskly through the day, preserve my hard-earned cash, and meet my own needs. And yes, these things have their importance, but the moment I fail to notice my empathy stagnating, I know, with all my heart, that something has gone terribly wrong.

ON THE OTHER SIDE

A friend of mine, a Special Forces commander with the US Army, has seen things no one should ever have to see. He's done things that no one should ever have to do. I once admitted to him that although I'd never wished to take part in a battle, it sometimes feels that never having had that experience may have left a kind of hole in my life. My friend told me not to worry about such things. "Being in a firefight, taking the life of another human being, is itself a hole in one's life."

He then mentioned something he learned from one of the soldiers under his command. "He was not afraid to die," my friend said. "I could see it in his eyes. I could feel it in his presence. He wasn't cruel or insane; he just had an unusually high degree of faith." Hardly a day goes by when I don't consider what that fearless soldier told my friend next. "The same God that protects and comforts me on this side of the veil will protect and comfort me on the other side as well."

THE DELICATE
INDESTRUCTIBILITY OF LOVE

I'm leaving for Chicago today. That means I'll be making a
stop at LAX, the Los Angeles International Airport, a place
that's not really a place at all. It is, like every other large airport, merely a transit hub. Every moment spent there is like
being thrust onto a conveyor belt inside a sprawling and
ungainly machine.

There's an elderly couple stopped alongside me in the
security line. The man is tall with thinning gray hair. He walks
with a cane. The woman is tall as well. She appears digni-
fied even as she leans on a cane of her own. There's nothing
unusual about the two of them, yet I'm struck by the concern
they seem to have for each other. They seem adrift here; their
faces bear expressions of slight panic. The primal need these
two seem to have for each other is what first makes me take
notice of them.

How is it, I wonder, that people stay together so many
years after the infatuation of first love is gone? Divorce won't
come for this couple; they're much too old for that now.
They've made it past countless fraught times, times when they
might have followed their baser instincts. But what, then, is

the glue that despite those tensions keeps this couple bound to each other?

The woman reaches into her bag and hands the man her water bottle. He takes a sip and tenderly wraps his arm around her shoulders. He whispers something in her ear, and she smiles. Watching them as they make their way slowly through the line, up to the gate, and later onto the plane is as significant a moment as I've had in a long time.

This elderly couple is a manifestation of something exceptional. Their love and care for each other is instructive.

Earlier, I mentioned how the 99.9 percent material makeup of humankind appears to dominate—at least, quantitatively—over the 0.1 percent spiritual. The moment shows me, as only things of great beauty can, the eventual primacy of the spiritual over the material. I believe that God guides us to the places we find ourselves not simply for the obvious reasons but also for the essential reasons. It's easy to see that I was sent to LAX this morning not just to catch a flight to Chicago but also to catch a glimpse of the delicate indestructibility of love.

WISHING YOU WERE
SOMEPLACE ELSE
(NOTE TO SELF)

This morning you were on hold waiting for a "representative" to help you with a billing issue while a loop of horrible music played. Later, you were inwardly groaning during a long and stultifying virtual meeting. Toward evening you were waiting in an endless slog of rush-hour traffic. In each of those moments you caught yourself complaining, wishing you were someplace else. But tonight, just as you were falling asleep, you couldn't help thinking back to what you'd experienced that day, especially in those empty moments. And somewhere between sleep and dreaming, you were struck by a simple idea:

Aren't those experiences—the waiting, the groaning, the slogging, the complaining—also the hours and minutes of my life? Aren't they also the precious, fleeting events of my measured days?

SEVEN QUALITIES FOUND ONLY IN GOD

Rabbeinu Bachya ibn Pekudah, an eleventh-century Spanish philosopher and rabbi, listed these seven attributes of God in his renowned work *Gate of Trust*, which has been used for centuries as a tool for the development of reliance on God.

1. God has compassion for His creation.

2. God does not ignore those He cares for.

3. God is all-knowing and invincible.

4. God knows what's best for us.

5. God is the only one who takes care of us.

6. The things that benefit us, as well as the things that harm us, are solely in the hands of God.

7. God's goodwill extends to everything He created.

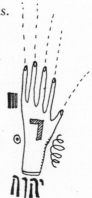

AMEN

I recall a time years ago when I was working through a host of issues ranging from the dissolution of a long-term relationship to problems I'd been having in my career. I had a conversation with a close friend and wise mentor then. His first response to solving my problems had been to think of things he could say to cheer me up.

"You've got a lot of people who love and care for you."

"Maybe you could consider this challenging time an opportunity for growth."

"Don't feel down; time heals everything."

Then he abruptly stopped that train of thought and offered me a blessing.

"May you experience stupendous levels of joy and love. And starting from today, may the next years of your life be filled with an abundance of health, wealth, strength, and vitality."

I was unmoved.

I recall my friend saying, "I know you don't feel any different now from the way you did a second ago, but that's not the point. The point is that those good wishes have been planted in you like a seed. If you're willing to accept them on *any* level, that seed will have a chance to blossom. Just say 'amen,' and it will signify your acceptance of my blessing."

Not quite knowing if he was serious or not, I said, "Amen."

Looking back, I can't say whether the blessing *worked*, but I know that I began to see my issues with greater clarity. As a result, I took the appropriate steps to deal with them. And I also know that little by little, things began to change for the better.

❏ ❏ ❏

"Amen" is an acronym for the Hebrew words *El Melech ne'eman*, which mean "God is the faithful King." When we say "amen" with the calm understanding that God is, indeed, the ruler of the universe, we will have the confidence to act in ways that are likely to manifest the blessings we've received.

אמן

EARRING, 1976

Today I'm going to do something dangerous. I'll drive to the Ridgedale Mall, walk into Now and Then, and ask to have my ear pierced. First, I'll go see my dad at his office to notify him of my plan. I'm sure he won't be happy. Ex-Marines hate earrings.

"Wow, that's great, Pete," he says. "Which ear are you gonna pierce?"

"Uhhh, my right ear, I guess." His enthusiasm catches me by surprise.

"Are you gonna get a hoop or a stud?"

What's remarkable, I think, is that my dad even knows the words hoop *or* stud.

"I'll probably start with a stud and then get a hoop as the ear heals."

"A hoop is nice," my dad says. "How much is this whole deal gonna cost?"

"Twenty bucks," I say.

My dad peels off three crisp ten-dollar bills and places them in my hand.

As I pull out of the parking lot, I see him standing just outside the front door. I roll down my window. My dad is smiling. "Pete, one more thing.

"Don't come home."

MURDER ON THE SECOND ROAD
(NOTE TO SELF)

You've been staring out the window at some men working on the roof of a garage. You hear their hammers and their power saws. The sun is low in the sky, and just minutes ago a thin layer of clouds burned away, revealing a pale and beautiful blue. There are no pressing issues, no problems that need solving. But alongside this calm there is a gnawing feeling of unease, one that's begun to splash a dark gray stain on the backdrop of your mind.

At just this instant, you've found yourself at a crossroads. One of those roads leads you to an easy feeling, a sense of trust that all will be well. The other road leads you to thoughts of despair. Why, you wonder, is that second road so much more enticing, so much easier to pursue? And so you do just that. You follow that second road.

It's not as if you've fallen off the edge of the world; everything is as it was. You can still hear the hammers pounding and the saws grinding away. You continue to see the sun shining in the watery blue of the sky, along with the occasional seabird or butterfly that floats past your window. But as you watch the men pause to sip their coffee and smoke their cigarettes, you suddenly realize that you've been overtaken by a sense of dread.

Oh my God, you think. I'm literally killing time!

WINGED WORDS

I walked down to the beach this morning, past opulent homes that look out over Santa Monica Bay. I saw a dozen or so highway maintenance workers walking to their jobs. I imagined I could see what they were seeing—unattainable wealth; an excess of things; a languid inertia, all in a vaguely hostile environment where people don't deign to clean their own toilets. As I watched the workers drink their coffee and speak on their cell phones, I imagined the connections they had with the people they love, people with whom they share a language and a common story. And suddenly I thought, *Who shares my language? Who understands the way I see things? Who knows my history—knows the things that bore me, the things that excite me, the things I find offensive, and the things that move me to tears? Whom can I be myself around, and whom can I trust? I can see their faces. They are so few.*

When our youngest child, Josiah, was around six years old, I once asked him to tell me the names of people he really trusted, people he felt he could be completely comfortable with. He named everyone in our immediate family—my mom, my brother, my sisters, and then he paused. "I also like Peter Weintraub," he said, referring to a family friend.

How did Josiah know that Peter was, indeed, a trustworthy man, a good man? I never spoke to him about Peter, nor did Josiah ever mention him to me. The idea that someone so young can sense decency in a person is itself mysterious. It must have been something in Peter's language. As I looked back on the uplifting things he'd say, it seemed to me that his language was made of wings.

"I'm happy you're here."

"Do you need anything?"

"Are you okay?"

Words so pure that even a child of six hears them and immediately feels better about his place in the world.

STUFF WE "KNOW"

Tell me what you know about carrots.

Carrots…well, I'm not a botanist, but I'll give it my best shot. First, carrots are mostly orange, although I've seen purple carrots and white ones that look like skinny parsnips.

Great. Go on.

I like them, generally speaking. They're crunchy, unless of course they've been boiled. I don't particularly care for the boiled ones. Carrots are also good for one's eyesight. They contain vitamin A—or is it D? I can never remember.

Tell me more.

Let me think. They also contain beta-carotene—that's the source of their vitamin content, and it might have something to do with why they're called carrots, although I can't be sure. It sounds right, though. Carrots are root vegetables, which means that, like potatoes and beets, they grow underground. The underground part is what we usually eat. But the carrot tops, the green parts, stay above ground. The green parts are vital to the health of the carrot because they use a process called photosynthesis to transform sunlight into energy for the carrot's growth—it's a process that's vital to all plants.

You really do know a lot about carrots. Where do they come from?

I just told you: they come from the soil, especially from fertile soil, capable of growing carrots.

Where does the soil come from?

It comes from the dissolution and disintegration of rocks, minerals, plant matter, and animal matter.

That's a lot of information. Let's take just one piece. Where do rocks come from?

They've broken off of larger rocks—mountains, too, if you want to go way back.

I see. And where do mountains come from?

They come from the shifting of tectonic plates far beneath the surface of the earth.

Interesting. And where did those tectonic plates come from?

The plates are just part of the earth, which I once read is close to four and a half billion years old.

And where did the earth come from?

It broke off of a larger planet.

And where did that planet come from?

Well, again, it's likely that it broke off of an even larger planet.

And that one, the even larger planet...

◻ ◻ ◻

An anthropologist once asked a tribal elder how he thought the earth suspended itself in space. "It rests on the back of a giant turtle," the elder said.

"And can you tell me what's under the turtle?" the anthropologist asked.

"Another turtle," said the elder.

"And under that turtle?" pressed the anthropologist.

Frustrated with the questions, the elder shot back, "It's turtles all the way down!"

WHAT IN THE WORLD IS CERTAIN ABOUT THE WORLD?
(NOTE TO SELF)

Two crows streak out of the pole barn, screeching as they fly up past the naked maple trees. A layer of ice has formed around everything—the tall grass that remains standing even after three days of snowfall, the decaying husks of the cattails near the frozen pond, the stubborn leaves of the birch trees that steadfastly refuse to fall. In every direction, the world is encased in what looks like a sheath of glass. Now, as the wind whips up, the sky changes minute by minute. First the sun shimmers alone in a vast sea of blue. Then a solemn bank of mud-colored clouds rushes in to blot out its light. The air itself feels alive, formidable.

You're suddenly reminded of your childhood in the long, cold Minnesota winters and of the blissful lethargy you'd feel while lying in a hole you'd dug in the snow. You were reminded as well of your mother's admonition to never fall asleep in subzero temperatures. "Children die outside in the winter," she said. How, you wondered, could something so peaceful as lying in this snow—which, bundled as you were in your heavy winter clothing, didn't feel the least bit cold—be a thing that could cause your death? You recalled that you often had to decide between staying outside, where it was dangerous and surreal, and coming indoors, where everything was bland and familiar. Of course, you'd almost always chosen the former.

Your footfalls make more noise than you'd expected as you trudge through ice-crusted snow toward the mailbox, a quarter of a mile down the road. You're feeling the same things you assume everyone must feel when fetching the mail: *It's possible that today something will arrive in a box or an envelope to change my life, to lift me toward some better circumstance.*

And finally, as always, you find yourself wondering what this all means. You can't help yourself. *What does it mean to have witnessed those screeching crows? To have seen that ethereal layer of ice covering every exposed surface? What does it mean to have seen the sky change so quickly and so radically? What does it mean to have recalled my childhood—specifically, the moment when I contemplated my own mortality?*

You are sometimes too quick to need to make sense of things. *What does this movie mean? What does this book mean? What does this song mean?* And to satisfy that curiosity, you often feel like you must imbue your own work with specific connotations. "This song is about man's inhumanity to man." "This verse reveals the predatory impulse of the rich." "This chord shift depicts an existential longing for emotional attachment."

The meanings you apply are understandable—on some level, at least. But if you're hamstrung by the need to continually deliver or receive meaning, whatever you create or absorb will be lacking an essential feature. Like many people, you're stirred by things that feel real. And given that the entire universe is built upon ambiguity and mystery, it makes sense that only an indefinite depiction of a thing can ever feel real. Any truthful portrayal must be something that dares to encounter ambiguity, something that leaves you with even more uncertainty than you had before. This is neither dangerous nor limiting. It's how you open your mind to this humbling and humanizing idea: the world that God creates will always be unknowable. After all, what in the world is certain about the world?

SPACES IN A FAST OF WORDS

During the six-week period of complete vocal rest that was prescribed for me after vocal-nodule surgery, I noticed a very moving albeit very small thing that, if I hadn't been engaged in my fast of words, I might have missed altogether. What I saw involved a child of seven named Jeremy.

I was sitting in the synagogue on the holiday of Simchat Torah when Jeremy, wearing a look of distress, came running up to his grandfather. Jeremy could barely contain himself, and through his tears he blurted out, "Somebody kicked me in the eye three times." I glanced up from my prayer book and immediately saw that the injury wasn't serious enough to warrant medical attention. In fact, I saw no injury at all. Jeremy, with one eye closed, crawled like a tiny pirate onto his grandfather's lap, curled up, and quietly wept as his grandfather stroked his head.

Soon some children, possibly even the ones who'd kicked Jeremy, started up another raucous game of whatever it was they'd been playing in the room adjacent to the sanctuary. Jeremy, hearing the excitement, wriggled down from his grandfather's lap and commenced to play as if his eye had not been kicked even once.

The humanity, the tenderness of this scene is now part of me. The memory of it isn't much in the scheme of things, to be sure. It's not a trip around the world; it's not a profile in the *New Yorker* or a Nobel Prize. It is, however, because of its sheer emotional density, a dose of powerful medicine, an antidote to the endless yawning negativity I can scarcely avoid soaking up like a bath towel.

If I had been able to speak during the joyous din of that Simchat Torah celebration, I would most probably have been doing so. I'd have been looking around and commenting, sharing my all-important thoughts, and giving a full report—all in a spate of words that allows no room for spaces. Spaces where one can observe a seven-year-old doing what seven-year-olds do best, which is to display, in the most fearless way, their frailty and vulnerability as well as the unselfconscious strength that allows them to sustain both those things.

ON A BUS RIDE TO DENVER

M any years ago, I was on a concert tour in support of an album of mine. In addition to my regular band members, I'd hired a sideman who sang background vocals, had some serviceable rhythm-guitar chops, and played the mandolin expertly. He'd also majored in ethnomusicology at UCLA, so not only was he familiar with many different styles of music, he also knew a good deal about non-Western cultures. The band would leave each night soon after our performance to get to the next city, so we had plenty of time on the bus to talk about all sorts of things. One evening the subject of right and wrong came up. The mandolinist wore a kind of sardonic smile at the mention of the words "right" and "wrong," as if the terms themselves were I.

Because I'm a bit of a provocateur, and because I was truly curious about the mandolinist's opinions on the subject, I asked him what he thought of the concept of objective morality. As a rule, most of the truly gifted musicians I've come to know over the years are extremely intelligent, and the mandolinist was no exception. "Objective morality," he began, "is a fictitious concept dreamed up by white men to keep people of color in bondage. Because there's no such thing as God, there can be no such thing as objective morality. And just as there's no empirical proof of God's existence, there's no proof of there being any overarching rules governing what's right and what's wrong."

In the main cabin of our tour bus was a TV, which was playing *This Is Spinal Tap* for the umpteenth time. I stood up and switched the set off. "Assume for a moment," I said to the mandolinist, "that there's a group of tribespeople living somewhere in the remote jungles of Brazil and that one of their customs around harvest time is to choose a young girl of, say, five or six and offer her up as a sacrifice to their gods to facilitate a successful harvest. Would you say that's okay?"

The mandolinist seemed wary of an exercise like this. "If that's their custom, why would I have any problem with it?" he asked.

"Okay," I said. "I understand that you have respect for all cultures, but let's pretend for a moment that the idea we're playing around with isn't hypothetical. Let's pretend that we're watching the sacrifice on tape right now." I went up to the TV set and pretended to insert a VHS tape. Then I sat back down and focused my attention on the screen.

"All set. Now we're watching the little girl get dragged out of her family tent. It's just before midnight, and according to custom, the sacrificial rite needs to take place in a few minutes, exactly at the stroke of midnight. Can you hear the little girl screaming?" I asked. "Let me turn the volume up. It doesn't sound like she wants to participate in this sacrifice. So let me ask you again: Is this still okay with you?"

"I get what you're trying to accomplish," the mandolinist countered, "but it's a stupid argument. A human sacrifice would never happen."

"All right, I won't argue with you about that," I said. "But what if it did? Would dragging a young girl out of her family's tent as she screamed in horror be something you'd support?"

"In theory, yes," he said. "The fact that I'm a white man, born with economic resources and privileges, all of which have benefited me throughout my life—not to mention that many of those resources were acquired through the victimization of indigenous peoples—makes these kinds of judgments feel perverse. Look, human sacrifice isn't something I personally advocate, obviously. But I can't sit here and make proclamations as to its moral value for people who don't hold my opinions."

"I hear you," I said, "but let's see what's on the screen now."

The mood between us was no longer as playful as it was when we began. I stood up and pretended to fast-forward the VHS tape.

"Here's the part I really wanted to show you. Can you see that they've strapped this young girl to a stone altar? Let me turn down the volume a bit—the girl's really screaming now, and it's a painful thing to hear. Are you still okay with this?" I asked.

The musician looked annoyed, as I suspected he might. I carried on.

"Can you see the knife they're about to use to cut through the girl's chest? Next they're gonna pry her sternum apart and cut out her still-beating heart. I guess that's what they need to give to their gods…"

It was nearing 4:00 a.m., and we were rolling down I-70, around 150 miles from Denver. The band and crew were fast asleep. I sat down on the seat next to the mandolinist and poured us each a glass of orange juice. Not a word was spoken between us as we headed west. From the window we watched the sun rising wearily over the plains of eastern Colorado. The Rocky Mountains towered forty miles ahead. The tops of them were just beginning to reflect the rose-hued light of an early autumn dawn.

PRESSURE WASHER

I'd never tried using a pressure washer before. I'd seen them in action, heard the earsplitting roar of a gas-powered one, but I'd never actually held one in my hand.

Not long ago, I found what looked like an ancient pressure washer in a sagging, rodent-infested shed on our farm. I was doubtful that anyone could get it running again, but Gregory, a superior handyman whom I'd hired to do a few odd jobs for us, did a little tinkering, and soon there was a breathtakingly powerful stream of water bursting out of what looked a bit like a rusty magic wand. Gregory began using it to clean decades-old grime off the floor of a former cattle barn. "Give me a try!" I shouted, as if I were seven years old. Pressure washer in both hands, I set to work on the floor.

I was downright giddy with how easily it ripped the caked-on dirt from the corners of the barn. After a few hours, the floor, which had been funkified by large animals over the course of many years, was about as clean as a table in a not-so-hygienic roadside diner.

When I saw how rapidly a seemingly permanent stain could be eradicated, a metaphor began to form in my mind. How many of my ostensibly intractable problems could, with enough power, pressure, and will, be eradicated as well? This,

I reasoned, was cause for hope. Had it not been for the arrival of the pressure washer and Gregory, who showed me how to use it, I would have been fine with the barn remaining perpetually unclean—just as I had become inured to the idea that so many of the troubling and painful aspects of my life would forever stay as they were.

It might sound unreasonable to draw an important conclusion from cleaning desiccated manure off the floor of a cattle barn. But I have drawn one, and for me, at least, it is this:

I am no longer stuck in an untenable situation. Though I cannot at this moment imagine how my challenges will dissipate, God, who controls the world, can instantly cause positive outcomes to feel inevitable—just as the sudden and wholly unexpected appearance of the pressure washer, along with the providential arrival of Gregory, opened a universe of possibilities in a situation I had deemed impossible.

CRACKS

Engineers, statisticians, and data analysts can tell you about practical things. Poets, painters, dancers, musicians, and mystics shed light on the cracks in between them. Bob Marley, Jimi Hendrix, Jean-Michel Basquiat, Igor Stravinsky, Adin Steinsaltz, Joni Mitchell, Johnny Cash, Howlin' Wolf, Isaac Babel, Thelonious Monk, Yehuda Amichai, Jerome Robbins, Neil Young, Schneur Zalman of Liadi, King David, Sonny Rollins, Keith Richards, Menachem Mendel Schneerson, Nina Simone, David Grossman, Aharon Appelfeld, Marc Chagall—and a thousand others—helped me find what was hidden in those cracks.

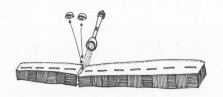

A TURNING POINT

In 1987, my friend and soon-to-be manager Wess and I were in Memphis to mix a record album of mine. Wess's folks were Bible people, hard-core. When he was a kid, they'd toss him and his three siblings in a station wagon and drive through the South, attending revival meetings and old-time Baptist churches, places where snake handlers and parishioners who spoke in tongues were not uncommon. "Welcome, brother," the congregants would often say to twelve-year-old Wess. The uncannily worldly-wise boy would often answer, "I ain't your goddamn brother."

So as a grown man, Wess knew exactly how things went down in Memphis, and he was worried about my impetuousness and about what I might say or do there, because I most definitely did *not* know how things went down in Memphis. One afternoon, while our recording engineer was working out the details of a mix, Wess and I decided to take a tour of the Graceland mansion, the world-famous home of the world-famous Elvis Presley.

We had just purchased our tickets and were standing outside the gates when I turned to Wess and said, "Isn't this whole

Elvis thing ridiculous? Aren't these stupid hicks making a god out of this guy?"

Wess, who was by nature reserved, became uncharacteristically animated. "You've got it all wrong," he said. "They're not stupid; they're just huge Elvis fans."

"Yeah, whatever," I said as we made our way toward the house, where our tour group of around twenty people was assembled. The first exhibit was Elvis's private jet, named the *Lisa Marie*, after his daughter. I found it hilarious when our pretty young tour guide told us that the seat belts on the aircraft beds were an FAA regulation and not Elvis's idea. "Yeah, right," I said as I looked over at Wess with a sarcastic grin.

Wess seemed concerned. "The *Lisa Marie* is a sacred place to these people," he shot back.

I told him to relax. "They're just a bunch of ignoramuses."

Back from the *Lisa Marie* and outside the mansion itself, I suddenly came up with a great idea for some additional levity. As the tour group gathered near the entryway, I made my way to the front, cupped my hands over my face, and pretended to cry. With a great deal of concern, the tour guide came close and asked, "Sir, is everything all right?"

"Guess I'm just thinkin' 'bout the King," I said through faux tears. "I...I just need to take a moment is all, ma'am." I snickered. Wess didn't.

After a few brief words about the need to pay proper respect to Elvis's aunt, who still lived on the property, the guide ushered our group through the front door. We found ourselves inside a bright green room with roughly hewn stone walls and its own little waterfall. This was the room that Elvis deemed the Jungle Room. Maybe it was because I'd just signed a big record contract, or maybe it was because I was mixing my brand-new record at a first-class recording studio just up the street, but I was full of egotistical insanity. The next moment landed me squarely at the nadir of my existence.

Without pausing to consider the consequences, I began reciting the words to the Beatles' "A Day in the Life" in a lousy southern accent for all to hear. To the die-hard Elvis fan, who no doubt knows every song he'd ever released, my brazen recitation of Beatles song lyrics, passing them off as something Elvis recorded—in the Jungle Room, no less—was the height of disrespect. "I will never forget Elvis's immortal words…"

Midsentence, someone grabbed hold of my arm and jerked me away from the group and into a faintly lit adjoining room. Before I saw him, I could feel his spittle on my face. He whispered, barely audibly, just inches from my ear. "I don't know who the hell you are, but I'm gonna take you outside and tear you apart!"

I looked at him. My assailant was a big man, maybe six feet four, all sinew and bone. His grip tightened around my arm, cutting off the blood supply as he dragged me out a small side door and into the parking lot. The hard Memphis light burned my eyes as I watched a single blue vein on the big man's forehead bulge with each beat of his quickening pulse. Seconds later, I had what I can only describe as a miraculous life-saving revelation.

Rising up from out of the mist of my subconscious like the headlight on a midnight freight train came this epiphany. You could say it was a silent, lifesaving prayer.

Oh, God, I've done something stupid and very hurtful here today. I have disrespected a man's memory in the very place he lived and died. These people have come here to honor Elvis—a person more talented, more successful, and more generous than I could ever dream of being. I'm the ignoramus here; I'm the loser. I'm the smug, self-righteous...

I looked up at the big man and said, "As long as I live, I will never again make fun of Elvis Presley."

He stared at me for a moment, spit once on the blacktop, and let me go. "You damn well better not," he snorted.

Back inside the mansion, I saw the big man watching me as I walked back to join the tour group. He studied me as I moved once more through the Jungle Room. He looked on as I pondered each of Elvis's outfits on display, and each weapon in Elvis's vast handgun collection. I was monastic in my newly reverent silence. Wess saw me and said nothing.

Elvis's grave rests next to his father's in the garden behind the mansion. It was there that I kneeled, chastened. It was there that I thought about the immense joy Elvis brought to the world with his music. It was there that I thought about his tragic end, at the age of forty-two, on a cold bathroom floor in the very house that was blocking the sunlight and casting its shadows over me as I prayed. I peered back over my shoulder and saw the big man hovering nearby. I tried to make eye contact, to show him that I'd changed, that I'd had an epiphany. But clearly, he couldn't have cared less. He kicked at some dirt with his bootheel, spit once more, and headed back to the parking lot.

THE INSUFFICIENCY OF WORDS

Yesterday began in a way that was notable only for its ordinariness. I'd taken an early morning walk, my mind a tumble of disconnected thoughts. The weather was on the cool side, and the sky was veiled by the gloom of dense fog.

Far out in front, I noticed a man walking toward me. As he drew nearer, I could see that he was using a pair of crutches. He was young—twenty at most. He wore dark sunglasses and a Dodgers cap, over which he'd draped the hood of his sweatshirt. Most striking, the young man's left leg was missing from just above his knee. I nodded at him as we passed each other. The young man nodded back. He seemed embarrassed, as though this particular stroll was among his first since losing his leg.

I thought about the young man's parents. I imagined how frightened they must have been. Surely, their son wasn't ready to go out into the world. He needed to be coddled, sheltered a little longer. But I saw the young man, I felt his presence as he passed by. He alone knew it was time to encounter his new reality, time to move, time to brave his particular version of the unknown. Humbled by the young man's fortitude and by the sky that had now changed from gray to pale blue, I began to cry.

We cry when we are toppled over by waves of indescribable emotion. We cry when our words are no longer sufficient to convey the weight of the things we feel.

WATCHING MY BROTHER FLY

Iceland's founders gave their beautiful country its forbidding name to scare away would-be immigrants. In a bid to lure newcomers to its harsh and barely habitable nation, Greenland's founders chose a name with a none-too-subtle promise of verdancy. In the sixties and early seventies, the "Uptown" area of Minneapolis had a similar idea. But its swanky name did little to attract the hoped-for shoppers and tourists. It did, however, attract hobos, bums, and winos (my dad's words) who began frequenting its streets in large numbers. Nevertheless, Uptown is where my dad chose to house his latest brainchild, Midwest Suzuki, Minnesota's first Suzuki dealership. Nowadays it's difficult to conceive of how ridiculous a Japanese motorcycle must have seemed. Only an entrepreneur with my dad's foresight would dare eschew the hulking Harley-Davidsons for a pint-sized bike built to ride in the dirt.

Midwest Suzuki soon made room for another of my dad's firsts: Tape Orama. The first eight-track tape store in the upper Midwest. The two businesses, now together under one roof, were officially and rather awkwardly named Midwest Suzuki & Tape Orama. Yet there in the small showroom were a dozen gleaming motorcycles, from the Trailhopper minibikes to the 250 CC dirt bikes. Along the walls, in racks ringing the shop, were row upon row of eight track cassettes bearing the photos of artists like Jimi Hendrix, Janis Joplin, the Doors, the Beatles, Marvin Gaye, and the Rolling Stones. I had no idea how my dad got involved in selling some of the hippest music of the day, but for me, a fledgling musician, it was a dream come true. My brother Paul, on the other hand, had far more interest in the motorcycles. A note to parents: Never bring home a motorcycle for your son or daughter. You run the risk of your child taking a short ride and then, like Paul, falling in love with its noise, its smoke, and its gut-wrenching power. Paul was the first in our family to ride the Target Trails, colloquially named for the Target retail store, which sat directly in front of them.

The trails were spread out over an abandoned wooded area, which had been partially cleared, leaving a dusty ten or so acres of dirt paths and scrub. It was the perfect setting for an aspiring motocross aficionado. From early spring until late autumn, those unfortunate enough to be living nearby would be subject to the high-whining daily, and sometimes nightly, racket of the bikes as they crisscrossed the trails. There were all manner of jumps for the intrepid enthusiast, ramps of compressed dirt where a rider could take on nine or ten feet of altitude.

The Target Trails is where my brother Paul first discovered what I'd interpreted as an unshakable confidence. It's also where I discovered—like any fawning younger brother might—my unshakeable confidence in Paul. I remember his smile as he gunned the throttle and made his way toward the Target Trails' most dangerous ramp. Gaining speed, he hit the ramp and soared clear over my head, his motorcycle roaring above me and landing just beyond where I stood.

Not long afterwards, we learned that a sixteen-year-old boy had taken the same ramp as Paul, crashed-landed, and broken his neck. It was obvious then that Paul's days as a motorcyclist were numbered. My mother had insisted that Paul never again ride his beloved motorcycle. Though I wasn't privy to my parents' conversations, I knew that my dad had put up no fight. Kids breaking their necks, life-threatening jumps that sent you nine feet into the air—suddenly none of it, including my dad's Midwest Suzuki, made a lick of sense.

The room I shared with Paul had long been covered with motocross posters. His dirty helmet was a fixture of our room, as were his scattered motocross magazines and his yellow racing gloves. Paul had even ordered a brand-new set of riding leathers and a yellow helmet. When he left home in protest over my mom's edict for who knew how long or where, his pain was my own. Even without a motorcycle, Paul is still the same heroic big brother I saw so many years ago, bike wheeling through the air, boots pressing down on foot pegs, body lifting off the seat.

And all the while, smiling for sheer joy as he roared back to earth in a haze of dust and smoke.

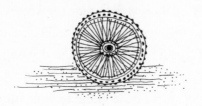

HOMECOMING
(NOTE TO SELF)

You hear your children coming through the courtyard gate. It's a sound so familiar that it's gathered in your bones. The creak of the hinges, the clang of the big wooden door being shut in its metal frame, the voices audible but jumbled; people congregating in the kitchen as they enter the open doorway of your house. For years that sound was routine: You heard it every afternoon when your children came home from school. You'd be working in your studio until you heard that gate, and then you'd come in to see them, to learn about their day, to sense what their moods were like, who was hungry, who was sad, who was excited about some small victory, and who was anxious about some looming due date.

Now that the house has cleared out and you and Maria are living in the proverbial empty nest, the sound of the gate resonates with you in a whole new way. Having your children nearby is no longer an accustomed experience. It is a rare and exquisite joy.

Today, they all came through the front gate as before, each of them carrying stories of stress and triumph. But as much as the particulars of today's scenario have stayed the same, the emotions that come to the surface are entirely different. What was once normal, once mundane, has changed; the very act of arriving home is now something of great importance.

The meaning of the word itself—"homecoming," which says in its beautiful, elegant way that there is indeed a place to come back to in a chaotic and troubled world—carries a far greater degree of depth for you now. Part of that depth is simply attributable to scarcity: When you don't experience an event, a song, or a person as often as you once did, you become more alive to it. You become more grateful, more fearful that this might be the last time. It's the attachment to people that interests you today, the day after Thanksgiving.

You've had an uneasy history with the holiday since Thanksgiving night in 1983, when your father died. For years the day has held a tinge of sadness for you. It has brought up memories of an awful phone call, an agonizing trip to the hospital, and, finally, an abrupt and sorrowful ending.

Today, however, just as you heard the front gate open, you realized that everything negative, everything sad about Thanksgiving has somehow been transmuted into joy. It's the joy of hope being finally fulfilled. You felt that at last, it was you who was coming home.

CANOE, 1972

It's only a few months before my bar mitzvah. My dad and I are paddling a canoe on Cedar Lake. He is an Eagle Scout, and as such he is in the stern controlling the direction of our boat. I am in the bow doing my utmost to provide the forward momentum. To the west of us are the homes of some of Minneapolis's wealthiest denizens. To the north, nearer to the noise of the freeway, is the purported nude beach. Every kid older than nine has heard about this fantastical place where you can get a look at real breasts, although no other boy I know has actually seen a breast since his days as a nursing infant—either on the nude beach or anywhere else.

To the east, toward downtown, are the rough gravel beaches, strewn with garbage and overgrown with thistles. This is the part of Cedar Lake where hard-partying indigenous folks come to have a little fun and, at least for an afternoon, reoccupy a little of the land that was stolen from them.

I hear the dip and swish of our paddles as we approach the center of the lake, and then the sound of men yelling from far away. Suddenly, a shirtless muscular man dives into the water and backstrokes out to our canoe. The other men on the shore crane their necks to look, all of them pointing at us and laughing. When the muscular man reaches our canoe, he grabs it and rocks it back and forth, trying to tip us over and into the lake. I'm terrified, but my dad just laughs and gives him a solid whack between the shoulders with the broad blade of his paddle, hard enough to matter but good-natured enough to show absolutely no fear.

The men on the beach double over with laughter at this. One of their own humiliated by two Jews in a fiberglass replica of their native watercraft is too much to take. As the muscular man swims, shamefaced, back to shore, I know my dad will quickly steer us to another beach and out of harm's way. Instead, he yells, "Who's next?"

Now we paddle toward the men assembled on the narrow beach, thirty or forty of them in all. When we reach the shore, several of them rush to drag our canoe up onto the sand. A middle-aged guy in a Ritchie Blackmore tour jacket offers me a can of Diet Rite and my dad a swig of Ripple from a communal bottle. My dad and the men sit on the uncut grass just beyond the shore. They speak about adult things. Subsidies, foods stamps, local politics.

With their voices buzzing behind me, I busy myself at the edge of the water, constructing a tiny fort of twigs and trapping minnows behind a seawall of small stones. And then, as the sun begins to lower itself behind a canopy of basswood trees, the men help us cast our canoe back into the lake. They wave goodbye and wish us well as we paddle out toward our car.

It's early evening now, and the loons can be heard above the steady drone of the dragonflies. From the north, I can hear the distant roar of the Burlington Northern line, which passes this way each day near dusk.

CALLED TO ATTENTION

In the fall of 2014, I received a scholarship to study at the Kellogg School of Management's Advanced Management Program at Northwestern University. You may wonder how this happened—it's not often that a musician studies management. But months before, I'd done a presentation for an organization at Kellogg called KIN Global, an international network of businesspeople, entrepreneurs, and innovators that caught the attention of KIN Global's founder, Rob Wolcott. Rob emailed me one morning as I was working on music for a new network television show, something far removed from business school. "Peter, dude," he wrote in his loose and playful style, "we have a fellowship we want to offer you for an advanced management program at Kellogg. After seeing what you did at KIN Global, we think you'd be a benefit to the other students as well as getting something out of the program yourself."

Having never attended college, let alone a high-level business school, I was anxious about what to expect and what would be expected of me. I arrived late the night before classes began. By then most everyone in the program was already in the atrium of the Allen Center for a get-acquainted event, drinks in hand, mingling easily. I walked in, and before long a guy named Steven Esses approached me with a welcoming smile. We began talking, and soon in his relaxed presence I found I was no longer uptight. It was as if he had somehow given me a bit of his own strength and inner calm.

From that moment on, Steven and I were like brothers. We encouraged each other throughout the program, and afterward we remained close. We spent time in China together, then he came to stay with me and Maria in Santa Monica. Afterward, he "pressured" me into joining him in weekly study sessions over Zoom in which we'd discuss philosophical ideas and biblical passages. The study part of our sessions usually lasted only fifteen minutes. The talking-about-whatever-was-going-on-in-our-lives part usually lasted around an hour. These were calls I looked forward to with great anticipation.

One week Steven, who was always on time, didn't show up for our session. I tried reaching him by phone, but he didn't answer. When I finally got hold of him, the news wasn't easy to digest. Steven had been diagnosed with stage 4 pancreatic cancer.

Less than a year later, I received a short, pain-filled text message from Steven's wife telling me that he had finally succumbed to the illness he'd been battling for the previous eight months. For a long while I stared at the moon-cast shadows on the wall. I thought about the details of my life, the unseen forces that brought me close to Steven in the first place. I'll never forget what he told me over the phone during our very last conversation. "I feel like this illness happened to guide me to some new level of understanding," he said. "I need to try harder to help and to teach, and mostly to become more mindful of the blessings in my life."

Of course, these were things that Steven was already doing, in measures beyond what most of us are capable of. As I looked at a photograph of him one morning, his smile beaming as it always did, I felt lifted by the strength of his enormous spirit. I felt him urging me on, asking me to do for him what he could no longer do—act. And use the power of my own spirit to accomplish whatever I can for other people with whatever gifts I've been given. I felt like I was being called to attention, called to awaken and take careful notice of the simple, often unheeded fact that life—for the living, at least—is always in session.

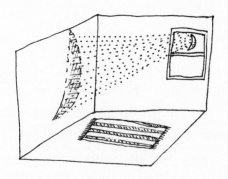

CHOICES
(NOTE TO SELF)

You arrived at the exact place you're in now in through a series of decisions. Those decisions weren't made today or yesterday. They began in earliest childhood. They were choices you gravitated toward, choices influenced by the people you were attracted to, the words that inspired you, the toys you played with. And perhaps most of all by the dreams that coursed through your mind.

Right now, for example, you are living on a small farm in upstate New York. You had been a resident of Santa Monica, California, for the previous thirty-some years, but in August of 2019 you and Maria made the decision to move closer to your four grown kids, who were living in New York City at the time. But it wasn't just the decision to move east that led you to this farmhouse on this windy hilltop. How many decisions, how many choices—stretching as far back as the first days of your long marriage—have brought you here?

The accumulation of decisions—which originate, as all decisions do, in the mind—lead to manifestations in the physical world. Meaning that the activity of your imagination will invariably lead you to real consequences. Some of those consequences will reveal themselves sooner, some later. Some are minuscule, others massive, but you create and shape each aspect of your life through the agency of your thoughts. The decisions you conceive and foster with your intellect and your emotions determine your fate. There are, of course, many things that will remain out of your control, but your ability to choose will never be one of them.

If you were to break down the number of decisions that led you to where you are at this moment, in this room, typing out these sentences, the list would be uncountable. It would include the tiniest things—the foods you ate, the friends you met and lost track of, the phone calls you made or chose not to make, the books you read or chose not to read. It would also include the most consequential things, like the decision to marry and start a family and the decision to release yourself from a major-label recording contract so you could spend more time at home.

The more you delve into the idea that—aside from God—you alone play the critical role in deciding your fate, the clearer the picture you will obtain of just how free you are, how independent you've always been, and how important each of your choices truly is.

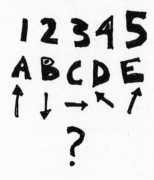

THE BEST KIND OF
SCHOOL BY FAR

Being married for thirty-five years and leading four kids into adulthood has taught me much about

humility

acceptance

forbearance

love

kindness

patience

gentleness

strength

resilience

collaboration

creativity

loss

discovery

memory

reverence

language

vision

persuasion

moderation

hope

freedom

prayer

forgiveness

dreams

elasticity

tenderness

communication

faith

sorrow

elation

endurance

becoming

transformation

openness

protectiveness
sustenance
optimism
God
and most of all
gratitude

A FOR AWAKE

For many of us, life can be boring. That's why we need to be entertained. To help people overcome life's tedium, I spent several years as a composer for network television shows, including the hit Fox series *Bones*. The concept of the show was simple and brilliant: combine desiccated or moldering corpses, ivory-white teeth, perfect breasts, witty sexual innuendo, and two main characters who in every episode solve crimes and come within a hairbreadth of having sexual congress. As an inviolable rule, each of the main characters' escapades must take place near the corpses.

While I was writing these music cues, I couldn't help but wonder why the people watching *Bones*, presumably couples in bed, would settle for this sort of wan titillation when they could be having real sex. Nonetheless, I felt I was doing something good for humankind: I was making life seem less stultifying for millions of Americans as I sat in a room for four years straight, six days a week, twelve hours a day (except for dinner breaks) on a green lumbar-support chair writing music to make scenes that weren't particularly scary or funny seem as though they were. Imagine the following:

Fast-paced action music for a drive to a bloody crime scene.

Spooky music written to make a not-so-amazing set look frightening.

Light music to underscore a darkly comedic scene in which the two main characters obliquely suggest having oral sex while a burned body lies on a gurney.

Sly music to propel a scene in which a handsome FBI agent offers a back rub to a winsome forensic scientist as a teenage suicide victim dangles from a rope.

Don't get me wrong—I liked scoring music for television, and I was good at it. At its best, it was a kind of lucrative puzzle solving. I didn't always do that kind of work, though. In my days as a minor indie rock star, I had the thrill of performing, making records, and hearing my songs play on the radio.

But there was a huge downside to that life. I was missing out on my kids' childhoods. I woke up to that reality one evening in Dallas around 1992. Sony, my label at the time, had thrown a lavish promotional event at a radio station for staff and listeners in support of a new recording of mine. In those years, I traveled with an enormous old-school cell phone—to be used in emergencies only. And that evening, just before our band was to take the stage, I got a call from my son Isaac. He was three years old, and I can still hear his voice, so sad but so determined: "I want you to come home."

It was one of those moments when I felt like something important was happening, something I needed to be acutely aware of. It was as if a gigantic letter A had been rising in the air behind me. And it was: A for Auspicious. A for Arresting. A for Awake. Not long after that night, I slowed down my touring schedule and got involved in scoring television shows, a job that allowed me to be home with my family for dinner almost every evening.

◻ ◻ ◻

It was during the time I was scoring for television that I began to develop an obsessive interest in Daniel Pearl, the *Wall Street Journal* reporter who was murdered by fanatical Muslims near Karachi, Pakistan, in the winter of 2002. Among Danny's last words were: "My father is Jewish. My mother is Jewish. I am Jewish." But my interest in Danny didn't arise only because I'm an observant Jew. In 2002, the American zeitgeist was 9/11—all day, every day. The nation had been permanently changed, and Danny Pearl's mission had been to unravel the mystery of this great upheaval, to help his readers understand the unfathomable. His heroic passion for that mission would ultimately lead him into the hands of his murderers. It was Danny's heroism that affected me most.

After long days working on *Bones*, I'd read everything I could get my hands on by Danny or about him. I read the French philosopher Bernard-Henri Lévy's book *Who Killed Daniel Pearl?*—twice. I even started reading articles by Danny's father, Judea Pearl, who just happens to be one of the world's leading artificial-intelligence experts. Some nights, while Maria lay asleep beside me, I'd be wide awake thinking about Danny.

Here was a guy who was traveling the world, writing about whatever he saw and felt. But as I stared up at the ceiling, I also knew this sad truth: he and I could never have been friends. Danny was flying at a higher altitude. He was busy with his brilliant, life-affirming reporting, while I was making little snippets of desiccated-corpse music. I'd fallen asleep in every conceivable way. Danny, by contrast, was a guy who had that big letter *A* rising behind him like the morning sun every single day. I was sure of it. I'm not ashamed to say I fell in love with Daniel Pearl, a man who was no longer among the living.

One early evening in 2007, after working ten straight hours on music for *Bones*, I took a break to read some emails. One of them, from a filmmaker friend, had this subject line: "I think you'll find this interesting." In the body of the email was a link to an article on Bloomberg.com by a writer named William Pesek. The piece was entitled "Pakistan Is Macallan." The article was interesting enough, laced with facts about the ISI—the Pakistani intelligence agency—and the United States' investments in its terror-fighting capabilities. But somewhere in the middle of the story I found this stunning sentence about Pesek's relationship to Danny: "We first bonded over Macallan scotch and then music—a Minneapolis musician named Peter Himmelman. We agreed he was the greatest songwriter virtually no one had heard of and we'd go to Himmelman's concerts together, once making our way backstage to meet him."

I could hear a dog barking at the FedEx guy and the assistants in my studio laughing about something or other as I sat at my desk with tears streaming down my face. What had first felt like another empty day in a series of empty days burst wide open and spilled its secrets. I was awake, rapt with wonder. It was as if the world's pulleys and levers were suddenly revealed to me. I emailed Mr. Pesek just then. He responded by email in less than fifteen minutes from Tokyo, where he was working as the head of Bloomberg's Asia desk.

Hi, Peter,

It was an unexpected thrill to see your name in my email box—I've been a fiercely loyal fan of yours for almost twenty years. Really—thanks for the note. I am based in Tokyo. As for Danny, everything you've read and heard about him is true—an extraordinary person and a huge loss to this world. As I mentioned in my article, my last time seeing him was in a Bombay bar, and I'll always cherish the memory. Danny and I met you very briefly in late 1995 when you played at the 9:30 Club in Washington, DC. You graciously chatted with us for a few moments and even gave me a guitar string that had just busted. While Danny and I loved all your work, we always agreed that From Strength to Strength is among THE best albums ever recorded…Danny also had a particular interest in your song "A Million Sides," no doubt because he was a journalist. Again, Peter, thanks for the note and thanks for your interest in Danny. He'd be tickled to know you were asking for him.

Regards,
Willie

Just a few days later I found myself in Encino, California, in the Pearls' living room, laughing and sometimes crying along with Danny's mother and father while I stole glances at a large photograph of Danny that was propped up against the mantel of their fireplace. I turned to look out their picture window then, and it was as if I saw that letter *A* rising again over the low-slung mountains of the San Fernando Valley.

That afternoon I had awakened to the idea that the things we do, the actions we take, have a much greater resonance in the world than we can possibly imagine, and that despite the conclusions we may have drawn from our many fears and our many failings, we do matter; everything matters. I woke up as well to the idea that even the smallest things—the thoughts in our heads, the gestures we make, the expressions we wear, the words we write, the things we say—have a weight far beyond our limited reckoning. And as for things we say, there is a Psalm, number 126, my favorite, composed by the world's greatest songwriter, King David.

When we return from our long exile, we will have been like dreamers. Then our mouths will be filled with laughter, and our tongues with songs of joy.

This is how I hear it. We are called dreamers because we are, all of us, asleep—asleep to the beauty of being alive. The promise of the Psalmist is that an alarm clock will ring one day and wake us up from our dream, a terrible dream that says, "Nothing is real except satisfying your own hunger and slaking your own thirst." And when we wake up, once and for all, we will laugh. We will laugh because in a flash of light, the kind that banishes all darkness for all time, we will see how we have been tricked into thinking that we need anything more than what we have right in front of us. Yes, we're hungry, hungry for miracles. But here they are right now, all of them, arrayed before us. Each one silently wishing we'd take notice.

Being asleep and its consequences are nothing new: We are simply doing what sleepers throughout the generations have done. We reach for the wrong things. We reach for Netflix instead of reaching for our partners. We reach for Facebook instead of reaching for our children. We reach for our credit cards to buy things we don't need instead of reaching for our creative spirits.

Like you, I've probably been awake around 0.005 percent of my time on earth. It's not a lot, but it's enough to create a need. Because once you've experienced that millisecond of wakefulness, you crave it all the time. Unfortunately, I don't have the Psalmist's alarm clock. All I have is my love, my faith, and my music. But I do use them occasionally to try to make that letter *A* rise.

And sometimes it does.

DRIVE-IN MOVIE

The lakes and ponds have swelled with the recent rains. The air is redolent with the warring scents of ripening crab apples and blue-green algae. Tonight, my parents will take my brother Paul, my sisters Nina and Susie, and me to a drive-in movie. We will ride in the banged-up Ford pickup my father brought home last week. We will climb into the bed of the truck, which he has covered in sleeping bags. And in the languid heat of a midsummer Minnesota evening, my father will rev the engine and the truck will begin to roll.

Out on the open road, the four of us will lie on our backs and watch the stars slowly appear as a reluctant sun lowers itself behind the gently rolling hills west of Lake Minnetonka. The movie will have already begun by the time we arrive. When my father finally makes his way back to the truck with the popcorn and the Hires root beer, I will be fast asleep.

I will wake up the next morning in my own bed, staring into faint swirls of dust inside a beam of clear sunlight. And just as I have no memory of my spirit descending to this earthly plane on the day I was born, I will have no memory of having been carried to bed in the strong arms of my father the night before.

ACKNOWLEDGMENTS

My gratitude to the following friends and family for advising, reading, and rereading my many drafts of this book.

Laurie Sandell, Jim Cohen, Jim Hershleder, Michael Perman, Mike Frick, Jeff Victor, Richard Abramowitz, Sharon Friedman, Lou Carlozo, Mim Kagol, Brad Keywell, Meir and Sarah Ossey, Alex Poltorak, Joe Heimlich, Janet Byrne, Arthur Himmelman, Josiah Himmelman, Khaya Himmelman, Raina Agi, Isaac Himmelman, Maria Himmelman, Chava Floryn, Michael Rothman, Doug Wheeler, and Michael Skakun.

Many thanks to Caitlyn Limbaugh for her wise editorial help. Her finishing touches brought the book to a level that I could have only hoped for.

A note of gratitude to Gretchen Young for understanding the potential of this book. In addition to some crucial suggestions regarding the book's structure, I am deeply appreciative of our burgeoning friendship.

Finally, much is owed to my dear friend and editor Barbara Clark. It's been several years now since I presented her with an iteration of a manuscript I'd been working on. The book was intended to be a follow up to *Let Me Out*, a book about creative resilience that was published in 2016. After reading it, Barbara delivered her verdict: "This isn't a book about creativity; this is a book about spirituality, about faith." A single sentence can sometimes open up a whole new universe. That sentence surely did so for me. Her editorial advice was beyond important to this book—it was fundamental. Having never been to college, working with Barbara, taking in her suggestions, coming to understand from her what works—and more importantly, what doesn't work—has been the best and most enjoyable writing course ever. *BWTS*.

ABOUT THE AUTHOR

Peter Himmelman is a Grammy and Emmy-award nominated rock and roll performer, songwriter, film composer, visual artist and award-winning author. He has been profiled in *Time Magazine,* The *Rolling Stone, The Wall Street Journal,* and NPR. Founded in 2011, his company Big Muse, has worked with organizations such as The Medill School of Journalism at Northwestern, The Wharton School at the University of Pennsylvania, The Ross School of Business at the University Michigan, and The Clooney Foundation for Justice to help leaders become more resilient, more trusting, and more willing to manifest their authentic selves.

Photo by Maria Himmelman